I dedicate this to all the great women who shared their stories, allowed me to listen and wiped away the tears. This is for all the mums, sisters and daughters. Agnieszka you will never be forgotten. For Banubai.

Rosemin has been working in social justice much of her working life. She has wide experience of working in sustainable education, health, social care, development and global issues. Her particular specialism has always focused on inclusion, race, diversity and cultural issues. She has travelled the world, working alongside the most marginalised of people who taught her about their strength, love of life and compassion. She has previously published childrens' stories and academic literature.

Rosemin Najmudin

HOLLOWAY

AUSTIN MACAULEY PUBLISHERS™

LONDON • CAMBRIDGE • NEW YORK • SHARJAH

A CIP catalogue record for this title is available from the British Library.

ISBN 9781398449381 (Paperback)
ISBN 9781398449404 (ePub e-book)
ISBN 9781398449398 (Audiobook)

www.austinmacauley.com

First Published 2022
Austin Macauley Publishers Ltd®
1 Canada Square
Canary Wharf
London
E14 5AA

Chapter 1 – Injustice

When they say, "The law is an ass," it is definitely a misogynistic ass! Worse there are as many female misogynists, women who mistreat and abuse females. Life is full of them but prisons seem to breed and give power to them. The police force, the legal people and the criminal system, particularly judges are no different. Ask any woman who is convicted, they never want to be dealt by a female police officer, solicitor or judge. Add to that a different colour and culture, then enter the injustice system, because lessons about racism are learned or experienced pretty sharpish.

I can safely say that ninety per cent of women in Holloway prison were there because of a man, injustice and poverty. Ten percent of the women were considered highly dangerous, often linked to murder or had murdered, or were abusing women with their husbands or boyfriends. Adjectives such as cold, evil, psychopathic, having a personality disorder, lacking in emotions and dangerous were used when they were discussed. Lisette who came from Romania, for example, brought sex-slaves from her home country, most were young girls promised a lucrative job that would earn them a salary which would secure a safe and good life for the family back in Romania. She came to Holloway dressed in designer clothes and wore a real fur coat, though it did not impress us as we assumed she thought it might. She was soon best friends with Julia, who ran a brothel in East London. Julia was in and out of Holloway, came in with a suitcase of beautiful clothes, make-up and a prison allowance full to the brim with money, so she could buy anything and all the food treats she ever wanted. She always had a posse of women surrounding and following her who did all her bidding. Julia did none of the jobs assigned to the prisoners. She did not even bother to collect her food. The only time she left her room was on our hourly permitted walk around the concreted yard, no bigger than a children's playground, where she met women, made various arrangements and continued to do business. She did deals the whole time and she could get you anything you wanted. I did not approach her but she did try to get me on her side. She was smart, charming and quite harmless, unless you got on her wrong side. I was my usual polite and kind self, I knew that I should never make enemies with her, or anyone actually. I smiled and nodded anytime I saw her, but as I never needed anything, I had no reason to approach her and I made sure she knew that I was not avoiding her but that I simply did not need anything.

Holloway was all about routine. When we were allowed to mix with the other prisoners it was mad and hectic. We had three times in the day to collect our meals - breakfast at 7 a.m., lunch at 12 p.m. and dinner at 6 p.m. The night was long and lonely for those who were in isolated cells. I loved my alone time in my single room. I had started in a shared dormitory, we were all separated by colour, but I was the only Asian in a room full of black women and I soon found my clothes were ransacked, my few possessions and food would disappear. It was not from any unkindness or malice but more from desperation. The women in my shared room were mainly there on detention, so women who were found to be in the UK illegally and threatened with deportation. The women were scared, but accepted no nonsense, there was solidarity and internal support, however, I was seen as an outsider, of someone with privilege, opportunities and wealth. In many ways they judged me correctly, compared to them I was privileged. One of the women told me that they were just borrowing. I never complained about them to the prison officers as we would probably all be punished if I had. These women trusted no one, except their little group, they refused to give their laundry to the women working in the laundry, instead handwashing all their clothes, towels and bedding. The old-fashioned radiators in our room were constantly loaded with washing drying, and imagine washing sheets in a basin and then trying to rinse them in our small shared space. There was steam, that musty smell when clothes do not dry or of wet towels steaming and making the windows misty. We had access to cheap laundry detergent, so really a washing machine was the only way to get everything clean, but superstitious and misinformation made these women trust no one and hours were wasted on hand washing, and occasional arguments occurred when a woman jumped the queue to the tiny basin or when there was no space to dry clothes on the radiator. I hated this room because it was full of constant chatter, smells of food and wet laundry, the television was never off, questioning, crying and even wailing seemed continuous. I was relieved when I shared this with Zoya to find I got moved into a single cell the next night. I do not know how she managed it but I was always thankful and so grateful to her for getting this done for me.

In the morning we had to clean our rooms, sweep, wipe everything down and mop. Some women cleaned their rooms and never bothered to clean the brooms and mops they had used, so it was imperative to get in early to have decent cleaning materials. Then the store cupboard was open for 15 minutes, 2 Lifers, women in prison sentenced for many, many years were assigned the duty of handing out toothbrushes, toothpaste, shampoo, soap, toilet paper, sanitary products, a scourer, jay cloth and a miniscule amount of all-cleaner, washing detergent and cheap fairy liquid in medicine cups. An officer stood near-by, but did not interfere. Again, power played its part here, Zoya had pointed the prisoners in charge, so I always smiled and gave them my sugar which I did not need. I then got my fair share of the goods. I noticed the black women never did, they begged and begged and were always running out of the basic provisions. As on the outside, racism played its ugly role here.

All my life I had seen "aunties," Asian women cleaning schools, public toilets and even on the trains. I was grateful and thankful to these women having to do such disgusting jobs. Many of my friends who now have cleaners hire these women or women who are from the Philippines, Eastern Europe or South America. I always greeted the cleaners and treated them with kindness, and was glad that my mum and I never had to do such jobs or needed to clean anyone's home for paltry salaries. I never really understood why people never cleaned up after themselves, especially leaving dirty toilets, their dishes and dirty clothes strewn on the floor. In fact, it freaked me out and angered me, why do people think that they are too good to clean their own dirt and clutter? I liked cleanliness and a sort-of-tidy. In Holloway you got paid, pittance, but paid nevertheless, so women were desperate to work as cleaners, cooks or attend educational activities as these were the ways of getting paid, to do jobs, work or study. Very few women had any financial support from the outside, family or friends who would put in the permitted allowance into centrally held accounts that enabled prisoners to buy food, treats and luxuries such as toiletries, basic clothes like socks and underwear. The ones given by the prison were poor quality and synthetic. We had order sheets given to us on Monday nights to use our allowances to buy from the outside. These sheets were collected Tuesday morning and goods arrived Saturday morning when it felt like Christmas. Women would apply for any jobs going to earn a petty income, especially working in the kitchen as this meant access to the best and extra food. It gave women power as they served all the other prisoners and divided any left-overs. All the workers were predominantly white and British. The most prestigious jobs were in the library or assisting the education officers, so jobs like cleaning the art rooms or supporting learners in the various courses, but this seemed to be assigned to the better class of prisoner. As in life there was a hierarchy, race and class system even amongst the prisoners and in the prison system. These jobs earned a bit of extra money, allowed women to be out of the cells and opportunity to socialise.

Not all education officers needed assistants but everybody asked me to help in their classes, so after I had completed every course, I could participate in each one of them. I carried on to work and earned a lot of money as these jobs were also paid better. However, I never spent a penny. I felt there was nothing I needed, I felt healthier and fitter than I had ever felt and I was constantly spoiled by the staff and women like Zoya who gave me food treats and all sorts of goodies from books, clothes and writing material. I was strangely happy in Holloway, no different to how I had been outside.

No one outside knew that I had been imprisoned, my solicitor had told me I would get a telling off and community service as my so-called crime was low level, as I had never ever done anything illegal, had no past records and the prisons were overcrowded. So, I went to hear my sentence taking nothing with me, with not an iota of belongings and only two pounds in my purse. These days I was always short of money. So, I barely heard or comprehended what was being said to me when I was told that I had been given a nine months custodial sentence. When the judge told me my sentence, I was in deep shock and I almost fainted. At first I did not understand what this meant, my solicitor told me that it meant I would be in prison, an actual prison for half the sentence and then get released four and a half months later. She told me that as long as I behaved well, perhaps I would even be released after serving a quarter of the sentence wearing an ankle bracelet called a tag that allowed me freedom during the day, but an imposed curfew at night. As if I would do anything, but behave. Of course, this was no longer true, I was now labelled a criminal. I had been rude to a judge and was now being punished harshly, so I was no longer considered good or trustworthy!

At that time, I was sullen, terrified, sad and so scared of what was happening to me, so I did not tell anyone, not even my husband a single thing. He was working away a lot those days, we had grown a bit distant and this was useful in my keeping my secrets. I just felt so ashamed and panicked. I am generally too honest and open, he always told me off about these qualities, so I decided I would be exactly as he wished, quiet and closed. I told him the barest of information.

When I was given my first free phone card, I called my husband and told him I needed to get away and I said I was going to turn my mobile phone off, but I would be in touch regularly. From then on, I called regularly and wrote him three letters a week.

He was confused at first when I called, asked if we were separating and I said, 'No!'

He asked if he could email and why I did not reply to his texts, why the phone number when I called was showing as private or number withheld. He said he was worried and I told him not to be. I told him to email and I was touched when I was able to read these. I needed them as much as my freedom when I was released. When he did see me, he was amazed at how good I looked and asked if I had been on a retreat or health camp? I told him in a way I had and then slowly explained all that had happened to me and it suddenly all came out like an explosion. We talked and talked. Eventually I did tell him everything, little by little, every small, sordid and detail of unfairness came out and then it was his turn to drive away angry at not being trusted and involved, but a few days later he came back. He was kinder and more loving than ever before. My short time in Holloway has strangely made us closer and more in love. He says he is in awe of what I suffered and went through, he does not think he could have coped had it happened to him. I think he is right about this. I do not really talk about it anymore as I do not think he really comprehends the specifics and detail of what happened. I even question it myself. I am not sure if he would understand and in a way this story is dedicated to him.

All the women rushed to get breakfast when the doors were opened each morning, a choice of the cheapest shop's own cereals filled in small plastic bags and usually consisting of oats, cornflakes, two cheap Weetabix biscuits or rice crispies. Very occasionally there was muesli. There was shops' own white or wholemeal bread which had been toasted and coated in cheap margarine, one small carton of milk for all the tea or coffee for the day as well as for the cereal and a packet full of teabags, coffee sachets and sugar. These were items that could be swapped if you didn't want them.

I had learned that the communal bathrooms were cleaned once a day before we were let out for breakfast, so I cleaned my room early in the morning, then as soon as our doors were opened, I rushed, swept and mopped my room and had a bath in the lovely clean room. I always cleaned up after myself but others left used sanitary products or a rim of dirt or a bath full of hair shavings. We had to sign up for a disposable razor and you were only allowed 15 minutes with the razor as there had been suicide attempts with the blades in the past. Prisoner officers were supposed to stand outside bathrooms and check up on inmates with razors, but the times when we were out of our rooms were the most hectic, they had to oversee that food and supplies were distributed fairly, one stood outside the kiosk where medicines and methadone was dispensed to those who needed them. The few staff were pulled in all directions and so there was never anyone outside the bathrooms.

Women who had been in prison for a long time always looked great with their hair short, neat, styled and tidy. I wondered how they did this as we were not allowed anything sharp like scissors. We did have women training in hair and beauty courses who offered hair-cuts and colours, but these treatments cost a lot of our hard-earned cash. I soon learned how they managed. They took the blade out of razors and feather cut each other's hair; it was amazing to watch this skilled activity. The black women spent time braiding each other's hair and almost all the white women with longer hair had braided hair at one time or another. Hair, clothes and make-up were a constant theme of chatter and involved deals and bartering being done in order to obtain small amounts of toiletries and make-up when there was no money for the many to buy in from the outside. Small amounts filled the recycled medicine cups and were sold, swapped and bartered.

After my lovely bath, I collected my daily supplies whether I needed anything or not. The prison often ran out of things, especially toilet paper, so I was taught by Zoya that I was to take everything on offer or given out and hide any excess. Finally, I went and collected my breakfast. I took excess cereal bags that no one wanted, usually the oats and any leftover coffee sachets that I gave to Zoya. What I did was mix the various cereals, just to make it palatable, interesting and fill me up. I always just managed to collect my food and the bell rang for lockdown. We had kettles in our rooms so I had a leisurely breakfast and a couple of cups of tea made from one teabag in our tiny disgusting plastic cups whilst watching morning TV. One of the best presents Zoya gave me was my mug. I tried to give it back to her when I was due for release, but she told me to keep it as a memory of her and it is exactly that, I use every day. It says "Rock Bitch" and has a drawing of a curly-haired woman who does look similar to me!

In fact, everything in prison was the cheapest and poorest of quality. The food was basic, but usually more than edible, the women working in the kitchen ate what they cooked so that was a bonus, they made an effort to make it as well as their knowledge and skills permitted. When we had the money to order treats and essentials every week, they were the shops' own brand basic range and quality, but prisoners were charged inflated prices. Every aspect of the prison was someone's profits. I read reports about how much it cost to house each prisoner, and the conditions were better than any prison in the so-called developing countries, even in other European countries, but in terms of the facilities and quality, it was really shoddy and lacking quality so questions need to be asked about where all the money goes.

What did impress me were the people from some charities, faiths and education officers. These were people who were generous, patient and with qualities that far exceeded what I had expected of the professional people paid to work in prisons. These professionals were the only people I did not trust, the prison officers, police officers, solicitors and anyone linked to law-making including the judges. I failed to meet one who was decent, honest and did their job fairly, to me they appeared to be selfish, self-centred, manipulative, power-hungry, lacking in compassion and easily manipulated by those who were actually criminals, and often very dangerous ones. Or is it just that the law is just easily exploited by those who know the rules of the game better than honest citizens and those with money?

I signed up for everything on offer, all the activities, classes and anything that allowed me to leave my solitary cell. Usually, we had to wait a month to be told what classes we were allowed to enrol on and weeks passed before we were allowed to use the library and gym but I begged and begged on day one. I was allowed to join almost immediately because I rarely talked, had never been in any trouble, never complained and so this request was taken kindly by the therapist assigned to me. The best courses and classes like art, hair and beauty and pottery were always full, so I did all and any other course on offer that I could attend or was allowed on. Most of the classes, like learning to use the Sage Accounting package, typing for beginners, Using Microsoft levels 1–3 were empty of participants. I already had a good knowledge of these skills, but as computers had been invented after I left school, I had never had any formal learning or training in them. I did all the courses, they were courses which should take 6 months to complete, but I managed to complete each in days. I completed seventeen courses in the short time I was incarcerated. For all the courses we had to complete portfolios and this was hardly ever done, women liked to do art, crafts, hair and beauty or any practical or dynamic activity, but there was little academic interest to do written work and complete portfolios. I did them all and earned certificates in record time, so I soon became popular amongst the education officers, the teachers and trainers as I actually completed and earned qualifications. I was so well behaved, tutors let me take work as "homework" so I did all the assignments with detail, hand-drawn illustrations and in-depth research from the few books I borrowed in my cell after we were locked in for the night. I used card, paper, felt tips and other equipment that I was allowed to borrow to decorate and produce creative files of completed handwritten work. I was soon invited on the popular art, pottery and hair and beauty course because in order to prove their worth, the trainers needed statistics of completed courses and certificates awarded, and I had a reputation for fulfilling this. All of them asked if they could keep my work to use as exhibits and I had to agree as I never wanted to argue. I was often given treats like a chocolate bar, cake or a donut as thanks. Imagine being rewarded for doing what you loved, I couldn't believe my luck! I completed a whole dinner serving set decorated with elephant collage in my pottery class and this would have been great to take home. I asked to have them ready in a box when I was due for release and was told yes, they would be there, but when I was ready to leave, the pottery was not given to me. It was one of the best things I learned to do in prison, would have loved to have had it, but I just let it go, what was the point of complaining?

Holloway prison was a strange building. It reminded me of a cross between what I assumed a psychiatric hospital would look like and one of those old-fashioned primary schools with endless corridors with tall painted brick walls covered in glinting white oil paint. It was hard to gauge how many women were held within these walls as we were divided into sections so the only time, we saw others was a small number on the hourly exercise period or when we passed through various other corridors to reach the education area. These corridors were endless, we had to wait for connecting doors to be opened, walk through, queue, locked behind us, walk through, wait, another door was opened for us to walk through, queue, but all this time allowed us to have a catch-up with others and again deals were done. I saw covert swapping and passing of tobacco, letters, and treats. There was hand-holding either of lovers or just friends. Women exchanged rolled-up cigarettes or bits of make-up. The front of the prison that welcomed visitors and staff was manicured and lovely, but what we had access to was sparse and unkept. It was an ugly, clinical and an uninspiring space. The odd posters or signs peeling off the wall, were often home-made and on A4 computed printed paper. The smells were of lingering foods like cabbage though we were rarely served cabbage, faint bleach and of body sweat or cheap perfume. It was so noisy, with the odd shout from an officer telling us to "pipe it down!" It reminded me of the hustle and bustle in the markets in Lewisham or some far-away holiday destination. The noise was constant, women were loud and overly dramatic with excitement or there was a need to show off their popularity.

A few women were always terrified, especially at night because there was often talk of ghosts. Women had been hanged and buried within the grounds of Holloway, and tales were shared about seeing women dressed in white floating about the place. During the night, women stood at the window and shouted conversation, or some were heard having an orgasm and it had been during these times the floating female ghosts were said to be seen. I would have loved to be allowed to walk around the prison and investigate the gardens, but we were only allowed a scrap of a yard to walk in. Of the forty-fifty or so women out at any one time, about ten of us walked around the circumference to actually exercise and have private chats. The remainder congregated in loud chatter or hushed deals. If Kerry was out, she wondered from the various groups of smokers, picking up the remains of cigarette stubs to reuse as smokes. Some of the women swore at her and told her to move on, but she looked fierce so mostly she was left alone. She did not bother anyone, but she did listen and was quick to share what she heard. At times she had misheard whispers, but that never stopped her embellishing and then getting her into unnecessary arguments. She was always in trouble from silly fights and clashes with other women.

I also took every exercise or participated in every religious group on offer. I have faith, but wouldn't necessarily want to attend services. However, in Holloway, I became more open-minded and I loved attending and listening to any outside speaker or different religious gathering as it meant a trip out of my cell. My favourite were the very left-wing Evangelists, but hardly any women attended this group of worship. A few of us who had become close, but could not openly show our friendships as jealousy and power games resulting in bullying were rife, we arranged to use the Evangelist prayer group as a safe meeting space. The man and woman who led the prayers were the kindest and most generous of souls. I am sure they understood our plight and fears. They would bring us treats and fruit. They chatted, read to us, let us talk, listened and we laughed, and sometimes we all cried when we listened to each other's injustice, talk of abuse, pain, of lost children, pets and homes. The worst of the meetings were the Muslim imam and some woman he brought along. They were orthodox, judgmental and extremely preaching. They never asked us anything, were punitive in their actions and treated us as if we were naughty children. I only went once to their meeting and they would come to visit my cell, asking me why I did not return, never waited for an answer, but preached and suggested I atoned. I didn't like them, but knew better than be rude even to them. I also liked the Hari Krishnas. Again, none of the regular prisoners attended this group of worshippers, so this was another opportunity for my social group of women friends to meet within Holloway. They always gave us strange vegan food, but brought us amazing fruit and sweets that had a semblance of Indianness. They were kind, sang and let us talk. I really liked them and the Evangelists.

We also met at the gym, I had never ever been to a gym before, Holloway also had a swimming pool and it was hot and brilliant. There was bullying and being petite, we, the shy, quiet and kind women were guided by the lovely Zoya to become fit and strong. I loved the gym, we chatted, listened to music whilst we exercised and encouraged each other to push ourselves that much more, to stay a minute longer on each of the machines and try to lift that extra weight. Then we swam, most of the prisoners would not use the swimming pool because we had to wear used swimming costumes and there were stories of women having sex and of course peeing in the pool. I never ever put my face into the water in the pool but I loved the pool. I was too small for any of the swimming costumes to fit me, but one of my friends either tied the straps or pinned them on themselves using safety pins from the first aid kit so that at least I was not exposing any part of me as the straps slid down my arms. For us, it was an area of safety and friendship, and this was far stronger than the other rumours that might have stopped us using the pool. Afterwards we were able to have long and leisurely showers in the clean and hardly-used changing rooms. It was all a win-win situation.

I remember the numbing first day after being sentenced, hand-cuffed to a prison guard at the court, taken first to the basement of the court where the exit to the outside was and being driven away in the strangest prison van which locks you in solitary booths. They have no safety belts to prevent suicide attempts, so you got banged from side to side at every brake and when the van turned left or right. We entered a huge gate and were met by prison officers who took you into a sort-of-waiting room. I remember it was about 6.30 p.m., they waited until all the cases were done in court, so all the women waited in cells in the dungeons of the court buildings, were then collected and taken in the one van, some returned back to Holloway from the trial and others like me who were to be imprisoned for the first time. I couldn't talk, was terrified and extremely sad. I refused to speak to or answer any questions from the other women prisoners and any of the officers. I just couldn't or didn't want to talk. We were given a medical, asked to submit a urine sample and this was tested for diabetes and to see if we were pregnant. I still could not talk, so I was left to write the answers to the various questions on various forms. We were given a phone card to have one call home as all our personal possessions such as phones, purses and suitcases, for those clever women who had come prepared, were taken away. There was strict guidance on how much each woman was allowed to take into prison, so all the belongings were checked and anything disallowed was stored away. No food, medicine or unpermitted items such as jewellery were allowed. I never took off my earrings, gold bangles Mum had given me when I turned 21 nor the ring my dad gave me the year he passed away. So, I refused to take these off and I was allowed to have them for a while, but ultimately, I was told that they would be stolen if I took them into the prison. I reluctantly took it all off and I was given a sealable envelope with my name on it to store my jewellery so that it could be placed in a safe until I was released.

I had barely eaten that week, never mind that day and was actually getting hungry, feeling faint and desperate for a cup of tea. All the other women had been taken to the cells, but they waited for a counsellor to come and see me. Food was brought for me on these awful light blue plastic plates, drank from a tiny plastic cup and old washable plastic cutlery. It made the food taste worse than it actually was. I do not remember what I ate, but I tried to eat a bit and remember there being a dessert of jelly. A strong cup of tea was made for me for which I was desperate and grateful. I had a splitting headache and I wrote and asked for paracetamol, which I was allowed. I lay down on the waiting room bench, an officer came in and gave me two tee-shirts, jogging bottoms, matching tops, 3 large pink knickers, a towel, some soap, toothbrush, shampoo and my plate, bowl, cup and cutlery. I had to wash and use these every day for every meal from then on. The counsellor came and apologised for being late. I said nothing. She was kind, but I still could not talk, and she made some notes. Tears flowed down my face. She promised to come and see me the next day and this she did.

I was taken to a solitary cell and was on suicide watch that first night, which meant that a prison officer would check on me every hour night and day by shining a torch at me and asking if I was OK. I still did not speak and as long as I looked at them, nodded my head, they did not enter my cell and basically left me alone. I never slept well after that all the time I was in prison, and actually to this day. Zoya popped her head, looked through the hatch and said hello. I thought she was a staff member but I still could not speak. The next morning, she arrived with breakfast and explained who she was. She talked and talked, told me and advised me how best to pass my time in prison. I listened intently but said nothing. A few days later they moved me to the shared dormitory. Zoya came to see me and she asked me to talk to her. She whispered that I could trust her, her warm smile and that compassionate, beautiful face with her huge, shiny eyes did indeed make me trust her. I started to speak. She listened and gave me the biggest and tightest hug when she left.

Zoya came to see me most days, often more than once a day even if she just passed and said hello. She started to share as well as listen to me and I did not really talk much even now. She was to be my mentor the whole time I was at Holloway. We became close and mutually in awe of each other, I can even say a deep respect and love developed, nothing sordid, but a pure and intense liking of each other. She never forced me to talk and I think it took me those days to become acclimatised to Holloway. Zoya signed me up for everything. She talked and talked, advised and guided, knowing that I was actively listening, she told me what I needed to do, where to find everything, about the classes, the visitors, how to stay safe and tips on survival. She invited me to her room, she had a bedroom, a sitting room, a small kitchen with a microwave and her own bathroom. She gave me chocolate, she always had leftover treats from meetings with Hollway staff and she never failed to share these with me. She gave me a beautiful bra and some other new underwear. She managed to get me some lovely second clothes, how you looked earned respect and she told me to always dress well for the classes, to wear the prison clothes only when I was alone in my room and when we were allowed to go out for a walk to dress up. She advised me to never tell anyone anything personal, never talk about why I was in prison nor ask others. She told me to be kind and polite to everyone, but to trust no one, not even her. We both, of course, ignored that. We became close quickly, she eventually got me to talk by showing me photos of her beautiful daughter who was 6 months old when she was sentenced. She had also hoped for a big fine and community service after her ridiculous court case, but she was given a severe sentence. Later we talked about the racist and unjust nature of the law and we both agreed the law really is a misogynistic, discriminatory ass.

Chapter 2 – Sally

Sally was one of the most decent and kindest women I have ever met. She was in Holloway because a friend of hers, actually a friend of her son, had asked that she look after his belongings, a black leather bag which she placed in a cupboard in her spare room. She showed him where it would wait for him, but she said that she hoped he would come and collect it within maximum of one month or two when he had found a place to stay. He did hint, as he tried to flirt with her, that he would appreciate the use of the room, but Sally had learned the hard way, having had friends stay before who did not move out as quickly as they said they would. She kept her resolve and ignored his hints, a man her son's age flirting with her made her laugh and knew he was trying to win her over. Instead, she let him put the bag in the wardrobe and she forgot about him and it.

Four days later police stormed into her home, breaking the front door and frightening her with the large number of armed officers and the dogs they brought with them putting muddy footprints all over her lovely beige carpet. These dogs scared her own dogs. She was arrested when they found the bag and her home was left ransacked. The bag stored in the wardrobe in her spare room contained a large amount of drugs and some counterfeit money. She explained honestly that the bag had nothing to do with her, gave the number of her son's friend and she was asked to explain how this man looked. The police accused her of lying, she was charged and remanded in Holloway awaiting a trial. They said that the amount of drugs and money meant she had access to resources that meant she might flee England. Like me she had no past history of crime, a useless legal aid solicitor and she was in Holloway for almost two years before the police dropped charges. By then she lost her home, her job, she had two lovely dogs which were also taken and this was heart-breaking for her. Her family and friends told her that there were no flames without fire, accused her of being stupid and getting involved with the wrong crowd, even though she had not done what she was accused of, she neither bought nor supplied hard drugs, and had not dealt in counterfeit money.

We first met in the Sage accounting class. She was smart enough to realise that whilst she was in Holloway, she had to make the best of a bad situation. She was in a dormitory, so we never managed to meet otherwise, unless she sneaked into my room for a few minutes. Sally was a natural mousy haired blonde, motherly in nature which made her look older than her 56 years, and her face was honest looking with eyes surrounded by laugh lines, though she said she found little to laugh at in a prison. Initially a few of the women had tried to bully her, but the women in her ward were kind and they looked out for her. Sally was good natured and generous, and this had helped. This never stopped her feeling scared. She thought she would be out in a month or two, but the police took forever to investigate, almost two years to progress her case which came to nothing. Before being placed in

Holloway, she had been in the cells in a police station and this was awful, it was a bare, cold room and she had to call if she needed the bathroom. She was not allowed to bath or change her clothes for three days, until they moved her to Holloway. She had not been allowed to pack, she did not even have her handbag or coat when arrested so she had nothing. She was always in over-sized prison jogging bottoms and a tee-shirt. I introduced Sally to Zoya at the gym. Sally ate and ate, she said she could not help it, so we included her in our exercise regime. Zoya introduced her to a charity which found her some nicer clothes, most of them were second hand, but they were better than what the prison gave her. Zoya also told her to not trust her son and make a proper contract, to make sure her solicitor put money in her prison account and thank goodness she told her this, because when released Sally at least had this small fund to help her.

She always joined us in the prayer rooms and gym. Sally told me about her son, who she described as useless and had introduced the man who had left the case in her home and caused her all this upset. He was her link to the outside; he had managed the selling of her home to hire the solicitors and she had asked him to invest half the money from the sale so that she could buy a flat when she came out. She had sat with the solicitor and her son writing all this down in a contract to make sure she did not lose everything. Sally thought that her son could not do anything without the solicitor checking everything, and without her consent, but she later found out this was not the case. He promised to pack her belongings, he even said he would see if he could find a flat and move all her stuff into it so it would all be ready when she came home. He had lied about her beloved dogs, telling Sally that he had got

28

them back and was looking after them so that Sally gave him money to cover their care. After a year, her son stopped visiting and replying to her phone calls. Her solicitor could not locate him. Her son had provided the police with details of his friend, and then had disappeared with all her money. The police came to interview her again and said that the details given to them by her son had not helped them locate the man who left the case at her home. Sally asked the police why this was all taking so long. They never answered her. She never saw her son again, when she came out all her savings were gone, all her things she expected to be in storage were not where she expected and there was no flat.

After her release, I got one letter from Sally telling me she had moved to Scotland, and was never awarded compensation after it was proven that she was telling the truth. She complained about her solicitor mismanaging her money, but nothing happened and the law society who heard her complaint hardly seemed to be listening to Sally. She basically lost everything except the small amount Zoya had got her to put into her prison account, so she had to start her life with nothing as she neared the age of sixty years. I remember Sally sharing how she had been planning to retire and breed dogs. In her letter Sally told me that a charity had helped her get two dogs and found her a job. She was a housekeeper on a small farm. The family were kind and Sally had a small granny flat attached to the farm. They knew she had been wrongfully imprisoned in Holloway, they were good people and never asked her outright about anything. They invited her to dinner every Sunday, and never let her wash-up or work on that day. She helped with housework, the animals and the land. They had fruit trees and a produce garden. She wrote how she got up scared and nervous, but she was starting to recover and the work exhausted her so much, at least now she was sleeping better. Her pride and joy were her dogs, whom she walked for miles on any free time. She told me she had not heard from any family and friends when she was in Holloway, and they still did not get in touch, so now that she was far, she did not miss any of them. Her hope was to save up and start to breed dogs, she thought she would stay on the farm as long as they would have her. She said she felt old, but at least she had become fit thanks to Zoya and was able to work and earn, be independent and have hopes. She said I could visit anytime, but had sent me no return address. I wished her well, wherever she is and whatever she is doing, I hope she is surrounded by dogs in a beautiful part of the UK.

Chapter 3 – Zoya

Zoya was the most incredible, smart and beautiful woman I have ever met. We developed the closest of friendships as only women can form. This caused jealousy in others and I was told that I had not gained enough privileges to enter the area where her cell was, and a prison officer came and asked me to stop visiting Zoya's room. We had started to have our lunch and dinner together. She had been in Holloway for two years, after being charged for fraud. She was Polish and worked as an interpreter. Zoya had managed to gain the confidence of all whom she met when she was working, and also in Holloway, was successful and had to hire extra Polish staff to cover the amount of work she was offered. She specialised in working at police stations and the law courts when Polish people were arrested and needed translation or interpreters. She laughed at this irony because when she was arrested, she realised how little she actually understood English law, how it was flawed and unjust. She thinks that a rival company had made up lies, fabricated and made a complaint and the police had raided her offices and homes and charged her with fraud. She was married and had just had a child, so she was shocked and scared. Being Polish she was remanded in Holloway awaiting her trial as bail was turned down as it was alleged, she could run away to Poland. Her husband was lovely and supportive, but he could not work and look after their baby. Zoya's mum came from Poland and stayed in London for a year, but she missed her home, family and culture, and then returned to Poland taking her granddaughter so Zoya hardly saw her daughter from then on as they used to visit every week. This nearly destroyed Zoya, but she threw herself at her work and mentoring within Holloway, earned money and with her husband's help was able to buy phone cards to call her daughter every evening.

Zoya was tall, had the most striking of eyes, long dark hair and the smile that reminded me of how Cleopatra may have looked. I guessed she was about twenty-eight years old. She told me that she had gone up two dress sizes in Holloway, but now she exercised manically, she was an instructor to any woman who chose to exercise and she completed more circuits than most of us put together. She was calm, polite and always smiling. No matter how horrible people were, and some women were bitchy, copied her accent and called her names just because they could, she ignored it all. Apart from me, I never saw her get too close to anyone, the first lesson we all learned was never to trust anyone. Zoya was kind to a lot of women, and on the whole she was popular, but she shrugged this off when I mentioned it.

She simply said, 'It costs nothing to be kind and polite!'

I knew this from life's lesson; however, Holloway was unpredictable and we understood that not every woman had our luck with loving families and a safe childhood. We never took anything for granted.

Zoya told me how angry she got, but she pushed it to the back of her thoughts and instead she did what she was good at, she charmed everyone in Holloway to gain jobs, rising up the ranks to the library job, became a trained mentor and also a prisoner representative and then an exercise coach. She was out of her cell the whole day attending meetings or supporting other prisoners. Zoya told me that there were some lovely rooms in one area of the prison where mothers with babies or long-time prisoners were isolated or there because they had a long history of behaving well or because they had prestige outside so were ex-police officers, from a good background or upper class. She was offered one of the flats there, but she liked where she was as the other rooms were communal and like me, she valued her privacy.

She also smiled and said to me, 'Also we get to see each other whether we like it or not!' She was a cheeky madam when she wanted to be.

Zoya's husband was loyal, but Zoya told me how her anger was ruining even this loving relationship and she just kept thinking that he is English, and coupled him to all her negative thoughts linking everything bad, awful and terrible to all things English. She knew this about herself, understood it was a stupid thought, but she never managed to shake this off. She decided that she was seen as Polish, a foreigner, not good enough and so she was what they wanted her to be, an immigrant and all she wanted was to return to Poland. Life in London had been easy and she had been extremely successful, but the jealousy and competition resulting in her false incarnation had destroyed her zeal for life. All she wanted was to get out of prison and return home to her child. She told me about her trial, false witnesses and lies about her laundering money and accusations of fraud that made little sense to her.

She described her loathing and hatred, which she hid from everyone, including her husband.

She had made regular requests to be moved to an open prison, which are much more lenient, allow visits home and a much better quality of life that would have allowed her to see her child and support her mother. Her requests were always denied with no explanations ever being given. She had spent every bit of their savings on solicitors to no avail. Her husband had to sell and move from their lovely home to a two-bedroom flat to pay for the endless legal costs and she was awaiting the appeal, but she had just heard that the "Right to Appeal" had been turned down and she was advised that there was little more to be done. She had spent almost a million pounds on the defence of her innocence and still she had been found guilty. She told me this only once, I could see her pain, horror, anger and never asked her any more about it. I learned that every woman had a story and it was up to them to tell you when they were ready, in their own words, most told you the odd snippet of information and there was no point in asking questions about their alleged crime. Instead, we talked about other things, often family, our children and friends, hobbies, and what we missed. I never told anyone anything about what had happened to me. Not even Zoya. I thought if I talked, it would all become real and I would be swallowed up by the pain and horror of it all.

Zoya had studied languages to masters level and in prison she was also now studying philosophy, economics and politics. She managed to fit this in with her already full list of work and duties, much busier than anyone else in Holloway. Like me she hardly slept and there was a lot of alone time. She also had a laptop, but of course no internet access, few books, but her course materials were excellent. She lent me her books, I read and we discussed them when she came to supposedly mentor me. I learned as much as her, we researched and discussed key philosophers, theories and practice. We looked at the economies and politics of major areas of the world and we applied lessons learned to the small world we inhabited. I read and checked her assignments, more for any English errors, then about the content or anything else as she was incredibly smart and sharp in her thinking. I enjoyed reading her thoughts and how she constructed ideas, her logical arguments and lessons learned into her work. She was very bright, intelligent and competent. We enjoyed every minute, even when we did not agree and she was stubborn when asked to justify and make changes, but she trusted me and eventually came around to my advice. I admired her stubbornness because it was borne out of learning, a need to question and logic rather than prejudice and fear, like with most people.

I was hardly in Holloway, and I clearly remember my last day there. Zoya made every excuse to see me, we ate breakfast, lunch and dinner together that day. She gave me treats, even though I told her I would be home the next day and she should save them for the many days she still had remaining in Holloway. She had collected an outfit for me to leave in, I looked like a new woman, no longer the beaten woman I came in as, but confident and proud in donated designer suit. The outfit hangs there in my wardrobe to this day, though I can no longer fit into it. She also gave me a gorgeous pair of jeans, she said they no longer fit her. They cost over a hundred pounds and I had never spent so much money on anything I ever wore. After the night lockdown, she came one last time, and they would not let her into my cell as it was late. She stood outside hands linked to mine through the small window hatch in the door, we chatted and looked at each other, until the prison guard dragged her back to her cell. When the guard came to get her to take her into her own cell, she slipped a letter into my hands.

She whispered, 'Read it when you get home, think of me sometimes and know I will never forget you!'

Zoya never replied to my letters, but I wrote to her every week, I stuck articles linked to her course, jokes, pictures and anything I thought she would enjoy. She denied my requests to see her and would not send me a visiting order. I called the prison and they said she did accept my letters. So, I sent her presents and these she kept, but I never heard from her again. I know that I have all her letters, we wrote often to each other when we were in Holloway, even though there was never a day when we did not see each other. I find it hard to look at any of the many paperwork that has filled one of the shelves in my spare bedrooms relating to my court case. I try to look for her letters, but then come across one of the files of papers to do with my case and I get depressed and give up. I know I have these precious letters and will one day find them.

Chapter 4 – Judith

Judith was nervous, shy, from a very posh, educated and a "good" background. I would have classed her as "upper-class". She kept to herself and was constantly terrified. You could see the fear on her face and in her demeanour. It was only Zoya and I who made any effort to talk to her. Other women called her snobbish or less polite names, but we soon discovered that she was just petrified, learned that she was bullied and needed friends. We found her to be a kind, thoughtful and gentle soul. We encouraged Judith to come to the prayer meetings, and she was the first to open up. She cried as she shared her unbelievable story.

Judith and her husband had two sons, lived in a wonderful and quiet town, but had a good life. She admitted they did have money, many opportunities, but were aware of their good fortune and did everything they could for others, were grateful for all that they had and thanked God for it all. Judith worked part-time and was a full-time mum, which she told us was the best thing she did and loved doing. She also loved her family and friends, they met often, went to the theatre, to the pub, ate out, walked and she said she knew she was lucky. She told us about her grandparents whom she was close to and how they lived in an exclusive village where house prices were unimaginable. They had always told Judith that she would inherit their cottage surrounded by land and this would help them and allow her sons to get on in life. So, after they passed away, almost one after the other, and got the stunning, but dated house, Judith and her husband decided to put an extension on the cottage to make it a family home and to move in as they had nothing, but wonderful memories of their times there. Their planning application took 18 months after fierce opposition from their neighbours. Judith and her husband had been shocked by these people who had always been so nice when her grandparents were alive. They wanted to be open and honest, they had invited the neighbours to a meeting at their local pub near to the new home with food and drinks to explain what they were planning to do, why and wanted to be transparent and clear, but hardly anyone came.

They had no idea why this was happening, so ignored it and when the application was approved, they started the extension work. They were served papers to stop the work accusing them of breaching some strange legal clause, and soon the police came to the site. Judith was at the site in a caravan managing the project so she was making phone calls to suppliers, arranging men to come in to do certain jobs and when the police found her, she was arrested. The people in the village were rich and influential. Judith was charged with breaking some obscure Building and Housing Act rules. She was denied bail and even the family's solicitor were confused when they heard this as there was no chance of Judith fleeing the country, and she was remanded in Holloway, she was also denied from being moved to an open prison near to her husband and children even though her supposed crime was not considered so serious that she should be sent to a category

"A" prison such as Holloway. They still visited every week even though the journey took several hours for her husband and sons to get to see her. She would cry and cry after they left. They were a broken family. Even her extremely good and highly paid solicitors were confused about what on earth was going on.

Judith kept herself to herself. She ate and ate as her only comfort was food, so Zoya and I soon encouraged her to join in our circle. She started to attend classes, we shared and discussed books, helped Judith to lose a little of the weight she had gained in the gym. She ate better, started to dress in the clothes we advised her to ask her husband to bring in for her rather than only be seen in the prison clothes; and we helped her to regain her confidence. She continued to be petrified, she never managed to get her own cell, and she was in a room with some unpleasant and bullying women, but she kept her head down, did all the jobs and managed to survive the year. She told us that the times with us made the whole experience tolerable and her family noticed the difference. Now, when she was due a visit, we helped her get ready, we did her hair and subtly did her make-up. She asked her husband to bring in some more of her lovely clothes which she now wore on a daily basis and she happily shared her healthy treats during our usual time in the Evangelist prayer meetings. She told us she was a practicing Christian and had always gone to church with her grandparents, but in Holloway she stopped praying and started to get cynical. I told her to keep her faith, she was such a lovely person, and so she should never let horrible people change the goodness within her.

Judith was released a year later and her case never came to trial, but the charges were never dropped. Judith had told us she would never sell the cottage, she wanted to be stubborn and carry on with the extension, but her solicitors advised her against it. They even told her to sell the place, but she and her husband instead decided to keep it as a holiday home and they never managed to complete the building work, the money had instead been lost to pay her legal bills. She emailed me a few times and we touch base now and then, but have never ever met since leaving Holloway. She has invited me to visit them many times, and I plan to go to the cottage with her. We plan to be loud and ruffle those horrible people's feathers. One day.

Chapter 5 – Dorothy

I met her in the Microsoft classes and she always wanted to sit next to me. She talked without any encouragement from me. Dorothy told me how pretty she was as a teenager and that every boy wanted her as his girlfriend, but her parents were devout Christians and strict. They wanted her to get educated and work before she settled down and married. Her parents were wise, they wanted her to have some money saved and be independent. Dorothy went to her local college and trained as a primary school teacher. She told me how she met her husband who had come to Ghana and swept her off her feet. She had been seeing a fellow teacher who also attended her local church and whom her parents liked a lot, but Kwame just had something she did not see in other men in her town. He was much older than her and had been close friends with her oldest brother. They knew each other from school days when she was just starting and he hung around with the head boy – her brother and the prefects. He left for England after studying finance at university and getting a first. Whenever he visited his parents from the city where he now worked, he made sure to come and see his friend, Dorothy's brother. He would then make sure he managed to chat to Dorothy during this time. When Dorothy was sixteen, he kissed her and told her what a lovely woman she was. He told Dorothy he had got himself an excellent job in London, but he would return from the UK and take her with him in a year or two. He returned seven years later. He came dressed in a suit and asked her parents if he could marry her, after inundating them with presents of a toaster and nick nacks from London.

Dorothy's mum never liked Kwame. She wanted her to marry the man from their church whom she had been seeing and stay in their town, but Dorothy was swayed by the stories Kwame told, the great life he had and how successful he was in London. He was only in Ghana for 2 weeks as he said his big, important job could not free him any longer. They married that Sunday in church and Kwame left after their two-day honeymoon in Accra, the capital city from where he flew back to England, leaving her to make her own way back to her parents. He said he would send her a ticket immediately, but it came almost a year and half later. Dorothy told me how she cried and cried when her parents, her siblings and all the people from the church came to say farewell, the family she left at the airport in Ghana said goodbye, and during the flight to London the tears would not stop. She thought she would be really excited to see Kwame, but his letters to her before she left her home country were brief, lacked any detail and showed little love for her. When he called, the rare time, usually it was she who telephoned him on his costly mobile, he was charming and continued to show off, but never directly answered her queries of when he would send her a ticket to join him. There were no romantic cards, he even forgot her birthday, Christmas came and went without so much as a present yet she has spent a month's salary on a parcel full of presents she sent to him. She had doubts, but she was now married and she had to go to her husband. It would all be fine.

He was two hours late to pick her up at the airport, she expected him to have come in the big car he had shown everyone photographs of, but they did not even take a taxi to their home. He moaned, complained at the heaviness, dragged the suitcases and her onto the underground. It took another two hours before they took a bus to the tiny flat in a high-rise block of flats which he told her was to be her home. Where was the lovely house and garden, he had promised her, shown everyone photographs of? He was in a terrible mood, the flat was cold and damp and she knew better than to ask him any questions. He said that he had to go and buy food, left her and did not return. He came back two days later. She nearly went out of her mind with the cold, hunger and fear. She did not understand what was going on. He had told her not to bring her old mobile phone with her, promising to buy her the latest model, but she could not find a phone in the flat. Dorothy had not left the flat, there was hardly any food, she did not have any keys and she was scared and confused. She heard noises and footsteps, and peaked out of her door, but never actually saw anyone long enough to ask for help.

He returned with milk, bread and a few bits of food. She asked him for keys and he slapped her so hard, she fell onto the floor and passed out. He shook her awake and nearly struck her again, until she cowered and this seemed to make him calm down a little. He made tea, showed her how to use the cooker, and he insisted she eat the sandwich he made. She was shaking and could not eat, but sipped at the warm, sweet tea. He then pulled her up, took her to the bedroom and forced himself on her. She heard him get up, dress and she heard the

43

door slam. She went to bathe in the freezing cold water, later she learned to heat some water on the stove, but that night she went to the bathroom and saw her body ravaged by bruises which soon became purple and black.

This continued for seven months. She saw him like this every two or three weeks for a night, two at the most. He never allowed her to leave the house nor would he take her out, no matter how much she begged, this usually ended with him forcing himself on her, a few beatings and the slamming of the front door. When she told him she was pregnant, he beat her badly, she could barely get up for three days, and she just managed to drag herself to the bathroom. When she spotted blood on her clothes, she opened the door, screamed and called for help, but no one came. The police turned up about thirty minutes later.

She did not understand what was happening, an ambulance was called and she lost the baby before she got to the hospital. A female police officer came to question her, but Dorothy just cried and cried. She was arrested at the hospital and detained at Holloway as an illegal immigrant. The police had searched the flat and discovered her passport and the visa had run out. They could not locate her husband, the flat was paid for by cash and there were no papers found with his details in the flat. They told Dorothy that they had located and interviewed a man by the name she gave them, but he was married, had two children and lived in a large house with a garden far from where they found her. That Kwame whom the police interviewed in front of the wife, said that he did not know any Dorothy from Ghana, had never met her or knew anything about her.

Dorothy was only in her twenties, but now she looked older and shrivelled up. She was a skinny woman, who spent many parts of each day crying or praying as she cried. She had been told that she was to be deported, but had legal representation and was awaiting a hearing. She had no idea what she was going to do and really just wanted to go back to Ghana, but her solicitor was telling her otherwise, if deported she could never return and it was better to leave on her own accord, rather than be deported. I do not think she really cared. I wondered if the solicitors were advising her so that they continued to make money from her plight. She had already been in Holloway for a year whilst the police had done their investigations and she awaited a trial date. She managed to speak to her parents a few times, and they told her to let them deport her and to return home.

Dorothy told me how she had not seen a single site in London, and had met no one except women in a prison. A lovely church was now helping her, different visitors came and prayed with her from there. They supported her, managed to pack her things which were now stored in Holloway and they kept contact with her family back in Ghana. They also gave her the precious phonecards which allowed her to talk to her family in Ghana.

Dorothy was released to the care of that church to attend her first hearing. Her solicitors said that the hearings would carry on for a few years and she could apply to stay in England on a temporary visa, but she only stayed two weeks until she could buy a ticket home with the money the church had raised for her, and then she left. She said she would probably never return to London or to England, she felt violated, destroyed and worthless. She wasn't sure how she would ever recover

45

or how she would face the shame when she would return home. We tried to tell her that this was not her problem and Dorothy said she wishes she had listened to her mother, mums always know best.

Chapter 6 – Lizzie

All the imprisoned women were terrified of Lizzie, even though she was young, perhaps in her early twenties, she mainly kept to herself, was often seen smirking, was quiet and distant. She was a pretty little thing and it seems impossible to see or guess what she could have done to get into Holloway. I did not know why at first, and of course never asked anyone, but I guessed it was something terrible to cause the rumours and fear around her. Lizzie was moody and in her dark times, she looked frightening as her angelic demeanour became more devilish and everyone avoided her even more during this period of time. The wardens and officers all seemed to love her, she was always getting special privileges, and she had a laptop so she could study, though what subject none of us knew. She was rarely punished or forced to do any of the horrible jobs. I wondered if they used the theory of "kill her with kindness"? She worked in the kitchen, the best job as this meant you got the best food, but it also meant that Lizzie had a lot of power as she decided what was on your plate and how much food you got. So, all the women tried to stay in her good books, at least to never antagonise her and never to experience her wrath.

Zoya had told me to stay away from her and I did exactly this. Lizzie never bothered with me so that was not difficult to do. However, one day Lizzie trashed my room. I had no idea why and it really upset me, my general way of being, my default position is to never annoy or upset others. I later learned from Zoya and I figured out that it was because we, Lizzie and I had our birthdays on the same day. I never understood why this would bother her, but I was popular with most of the women and so they had made a big fuss of me that day. Maybe because I was gentle and listened without interrupting, I had a lot of women who liked me? That day, each of the women had inundated me with lovely gestures and small gifts such as a share of their personally bought food, sweets, chocolates or little bits of toiletries given to me in recycled and washed medicine dose cups. Lizzie could not bear to share the highlight of the day, even though hers was quieter and with less interaction with other prisoners, it had been mainly the staff wishing her well, they brought her the cards and treats she had ordered. So, we thought that all would be fine as she would be preoccupied with her day, but when I was out of my room, I returned to find everything had been strewn and messed with. Her jealousy was apparent and she had that smirk when she faced Zoya and me. We said nothing to her face, although my eyes shone with tears. The prison officers said they could do nothing without proof, and let Zoya come after lockdown to help me tidy up. No one was going to challenge Lizzie, even when it was clear what and why she had done it.

It was several months later, when I saw a documentary about the youngest female double murderer in the UK and there was Lizzie, who had killed at age fifteen years by first beating and punching her father's partner to death, and then murdered her own father when he threatened to go to the police. A chill went down my spine when I heard the details and the way she had killed her own father, the life she had led and the way her character was described was no different to how she behaved inside Holloway. She was cold, quietly aggressive, had an aura of evil and rarely smiled. Her automatic position of being was that of smirking and looking through you in a cold and distant way. She was a curious thing, able to manipulate so that she could charm adults to fuss around her, and yet be cruel and scary at the same time.

I wondered why the prison staff liked her so much, but the documentary described her as "manipulative charming" and although it never worked on Zoya and myself, we saw how she managed to attract people to doing what she wanted and encouraged them to do her bidding. Zoya felt that Lizzie would never be released, but I said I was not too sure, it is costly to keep women in prison and once people forgot her and what she had done as a child, she would be paroled. She was young and I could see her living a good life outside in her forties or fifties. We hoped there was an opportunity to rehabilitate her, but she had and would miss so much of her childhood and adulthood, we wondered how she could or would cope in the outside world. She lacked so many skills and appeared to be void of certain emotions, morals and values. What was clear was that she would have a man and people who would do what she desired, and no doubt she would get to live and lead a decent life, even though she destroyed that of two people. We all have badness in us but what is the trigger that pushes some beyond the norm? If a woman kills an abusive boyfriend or husband, we have empathy, yet Lizzie was vilified at the age of fifteen. I do not think she was maturely responsible; I do not believe she was any eviller than say a manager bullying and causing immeasurable stress to thousand different staff for twenty working years or parents being so controlling that they damage the very children they bore. Circumstances caused her to be the person she was and society judged, punished and thought ill of such a child. Lizzie scared me, but she also made me think and question all my beliefs centring on forgiveness, compassion and a hope for better from each and every one of us. I always hope for the better. Always.

Chapter 7 – Tsitsi

I was shocked and beyond surprised at the number of women who were placed in Holloway on detention. Tsitsi was a nurse and had managed to get into the UK because hers was a skill shortage area. She had applied for a work visa, got it and entered the UK legally. She had worked hard and saved her money to support her family back in Zimbabwe. She was accommodating at work, never said "no" when anyone asked for her help, was a hard-working woman, and so she rose up quickly in the hospital ranks she worked in Lincoln. This made a few other white nurses jealous, especially when a few male doctors showed interest in her and her patients liked her because of her gentlerness. There was little diversity in the area Tsitsi worked and lived. Tsitsi never did anything to encourage this, and in fact, ignored the men, never dated, made it clear they knew she was married, faithful and loved her family. She just spent her time working, speaking or writing to her family back home or at her church. Tsitsi was beautiful, she was tender-hearted, warm and lovely.

She was the one who always cleaned up when some women did disgusting things in the shared bathrooms or the dining room in Holloway and no one else would volunteer to clean it up. If it was not cleaned, then we were all punished with our daily walks being cancelled or we would miss out on some other small luxury afforded to us. This happened frequently, and so Tsitsi started to clean up, we were all so grateful and rewarded her by sharing anything we had to give to her. I gave her my unused phone cards after I heard her crying after a short and expensive call to her children in Zimbabwe. She had left them back home, hoping to bring them and her husband over to England once she had saved up and rented a house big enough for them all.

One of the junior nurses had accused her of stealing and a few things were found in her locker at the hospital. She swore she had not done it; she would not have placed the things in her locker anyway, but the evidence showed otherwise. The police were called and she was detained in Holloway in case she ran away to Zimbabwe. She had been served with a deportation order, this meant that she would lose all her belongings as she would not be allowed to return to pack, she could never return to the UK and she would have a conviction attached to her name, even though she knew she had done nothing wrong. She was so scared, but she prayed and never lost hope and believed deeply in her faith. She never just stayed within her cultural group, she helped everyone, her kindness and belief in the goodness of all never ceased to amaze all the women. Some women had nicknamed and called her "Angel". Her qualities were indeed angelic.

Tsitsi spent about a year in Holloway before being released, but she had lost her job. Luckily some kind people from her church in Lincoln had helped, got her one of the better legal aid solicitors, written positive witness statements, someone knew a barrister and her local MP who came and visited her. They gathered useful information that later helped her case. The police sent the case to the Crown Prosecution Service, CPS, but they decided not to proceed with her prosecution and soon afterwards the hospital agreed to drop all charges and Tsitsi was let out of prison. She had aged and was nervous, but at least she was free. People from her church visited her most weeks, they raised and sent money to her family in Zimbabwe, they had packed her belongings and stored them for her, they gave her shelter on her release and helped her recover.

Tsitsi wrote to us and sent a parcel full of goodies to be shared by all. She told us that her church friends had helped her find a job in a care home and she had free accommodation with this job, she was in the process of bringing her husband and children to the UK. She had seen a small house she liked and her church would help her buy it once her family were definitely coming. She told us she felt blessed and God had answered her prayers. I had really liked this pretty, kind and genteel woman. Few women who have been in Holloway leave it and are this lucky. Tsitsi deserved it and I never heard a bad word said against her. I am sure our Angel is flourishing despite the hardship she suffered from doing nothing more than working hard, being caring, selfless and doing her job well.

Chapter 8 – Isabella

Isabella said she liked to be called Bella, she was an attractive, but troubled young woman. She often had tantrums, was always getting into trouble as she had the most parcels sent to her and she would try to swap her luxuries for extra methadone. Bella was young, but had been arrested countless times, she was always getting into scrapes, doing stupid things for drugs and the combination landed her in trouble. She was in Holloway for her third stint, this time because after her boyfriend had pimped her out as a prostitute, he then started to use her as a mule to carry drugs from other countries and bring them to London. When she was caught at the airport and interviewed by the police, she refused to give him up. She was addicted to a series of different drugs; her arms and legs were riddled with injection marks which she attempted to cover with make-up. You never saw Bella without her being beautifully made up, wearing lovely clothes and her hair done up. She never did any jobs, never attended classes or rarely went out to walk and exercise, and yet she was skinny and obviously pale even when disguised by make-up. She never really ate much as her cravings were always drugs and she often gave away most of her food. She had just returned from isolation, her boyfriend on his last visit had passed her drugs when they briefly kissed. The guards knew all the tricks, so she was searched straight away, and made to open her mouth, but by this time she had tried to swallow the small package. Bella said it was hers, so the boyfriend got away without being punished yet again. She got ill as she had bit into the packet whilst ingesting a lot of it, and was in hospital recovering. She was then punished by being sent to isolation. She already had a lot of mental health issues and never coped well with being left alone, but such were the rules. She did not manage isolation as predicted, on the evening she re-joined us, she asked for a razor when she went to have a bath and tried to commit suicide in the bathroom. Luckily as she was so vulnerable, everyone kept an eye on her, the alarm was raised by Zoya and she was found with her wrists slit. She was first taken to a hospital outside the prison, then returned to the prison hospital and was not seen for a month.

Amy, Zoya and I were allowed to visit Bella in the prison hospital when she came back from the outside hospital. She smiled and was glad to see us. Amy sat on her bed holding her hand and Bella nibbled at a bit of the chocolate we had brought for her to distract her cravings. She had not spoken to anyone in days, her family nor the boyfriend had not been told about what she had done whilst she was in the outside hospital and therefore were not allowed to visit her whilst there. She had been cuffed to the bed and only the nurses said a few words to her each day. Bella wanted to talk, she had not been sleeping and was feeling lonely. She told us about her last trial. She described how on one of the days during her trial, she normally went straight home after each day, but that evening a man approached her. They chatted and even when she told him that she was not at court for work, but was on trial he pursued her. He said he was a judge and asked her out for a quick drink. She said that she was told not to drink by her solicitor and he said they could grab a coffee, but he still took her to a bar and ordered her a double vodka orange. He was charming and flirting with her, but she said she managed to resist him. She knew exactly what he wanted from her. After finishing her drink, she went to the bathroom after saying it was time for her to go home. On her return he had ordered her another drink, smiled and said she couldn't waste it. He was kind and sweet, so she stayed. They talked and the drink went straight to her head as she realised, she had not eaten anything all day. He helped her to her feet and said he would walk her to the bus stop.

She woke up in a large bed and it was dark, it took a while for her to realise he was inside her, she had most of her clothes still on, her back was to the television, which he was watching. She tried to talk and he smothered her with a pillow, and she thought she was going to die. She woke up again much later with him fully dressed and shaking her awake, he told her he had to get up early and she had to leave, he helped her put her shoes and jacket on, took her to a taxi and paid the driver to take her somewhere she did not hear. As the taxi started, she felt sick and asked the taxi driver to stop. She got out to throw up, and the taxi driver drove away. She had no idea how she got home that day, but she did not manage to get up and go to her own trial. This did not help her case. She is sure that he put something in her drink, she felt terrible and much worse than after having two strong drinks.

Bella should never have been in Holloway, she needed to be hospitalised and supported, everyone knew her boyfriend should be the one in prison, but he was too clever. He had indoctrinated Bella and his other women to never tell the truth about his illegal dealings. She returned gaunt and pale from the hospital. Despite being abusive and aggressive when her cravings took hold of her, Bella was a sweet and pathetic girl and all the women realised this. She had terrible shakes, and many of the women coaxed and spoke to her gently. Amy was one of the few people who Bella trusted and she let Amy cradle her. Amy managed to get Bella to eat a bit of her dinner, and she sat next to her until she fell asleep. At times, Holloway was scary and there was bitchiness by some of the women as within any society, but there was also kindness and microcosms of care, love and compassion. Bella had another seven years before she would even be considered for any form of parole, I wondered if she would make it out alive?

Chapter 9 – Gurmit

Gurmit was another shy, petite and skittish woman, like I had been she was in a ward with black women, even though she was Asian, possibly Bangladeshi in origin and the only one who was neither African or Caribbean in that room. Hardly anyone spoke to her. I liked her from the start, I felt sorry for her, I found her to be decent, bright and polite. I couldn't imagine what she could have possibly done to be in prison. She asked me if she could straighten my hair, and I said I wasn't bothered by things like that, but she asked and asked so I allowed her into my room and she did my hair. It was really an excuse to talk to someone, I could see she was lonely and upset most of the time. She reminded me of a meek and timid little harvest mouse that I had seen as a child in nature programs.

Gurmit shared with me that she had been highly successful and working for one of the top London firms. She had never had a boyfriend, but was intelligent and successful in her job, just hopeless at finding a man for a relationship. She was desperate to meet a man, to fall in love, marry and raise a family. At the firm's Christmas party, she had worked seven years for them, she was touched when Paul showed an interest in her. He chatted to her all night and later he kissed her, he was very drunk, but Gurmit did not think anything of this. She was just so happy that a good looking and nice man was showing interest in her. A few days later, he took her out, he again got drunk, asked her if they could go back to her flat and she lost her virginity to him that night. She was smitten and excited, pleased she would have a boyfriend during Christmas and thereafter. He said he was going away for Christmas, she was disappointed he did not ask what she was doing, and she had hoped he would invite her to his family when he discovered she would be alone as her family did not really celebrate. Nothing affected her happiness, she carried on working, she started to make plans for when he returned and life was glorious.

When he returned from his holidays, he was cold and distant with her. She had worked throughout the holidays, her only joy had been to go shopping and she bought expensive presents for him and longed to be in his arms once more. Gurmit told me she did not understand what was happening and why he was behaving like this. His texts to her had been brief and polite, but she texted him several times each and every hour, the last one at night to wish him goodnight and she texted him immediately she was awake in the morning. She was so excited and happy. She understood he would be busy during his holidays and perhaps that was why he was not texting her much. She asked to meet him after work and he got annoyed and short with her. She had bought lots of food, had cleaned and decorated her apartment, was excited about having him share a meal with her and for him to make love to her again. He just said he was busy when she asked him to come for dinner at her flat. He continued to behave like this over the next weeks and months.

Gurmit heard women gossiping in the canteen the one day that Paul had asked his long-time girlfriend to marry him during the holidays; and he had shown his colleagues photographs of the girlfriend with the engagement ring on after she had accepted his proposal. Gurmit almost collapsed. She emailed and texted Paul again and again to ask why he had slept with her when he already had a girlfriend. He did not reply and blocked her on his mobile. She tried to talk to him at his desk and Paul complained to human resources and Gurmit was given a warning at work for harassment. Gurmit started to stalk Paul, not intentionally, she told me she was so angry at what he had done and she just wanted some answers. She just could not understand it, she was so hurt by what he had done, the more he ignored her, the angrier and obsessed she got. The police visited her, she told them what he did to her and instead the police gave her a warning. Not one of the professionals offered her any support or guidance, and she had no one who she could have confided in or asked for help. Gurmit said she couldn't help herself, could not stop the pain, hurt and shame she felt. She inundated Paul with emails and letters, until she was fired from her job after being suspended and humiliated by his representative reading out all the messages and listing her behaviour to the HR and her bosses during a disciplinary hearing. This made her even more desperate and she continued to follow every social media information she could find on him. She found out that he was planning his wedding. When Paul married his girlfriend, Gurmit turned up at the wedding. She only now realises how depressed and hurt she had been, Paul called the police and she was arrested and charged.

Gurmit was released on bail with a restraint order preventing her going anywhere near Paul, but she ignored this. She knew Paul was going to Argentina on honeymoon and she followed them there. Paul saw her at his hotel, took her photographs for evidence to show she was continuing to harass him and left for another resort. When he returned home, he told the police what Gurmit had done, the police rearrested Gurmit, she was imprisoned for breaking bail conditions and she was in Holloway on remand, even though she pleaded guilty. She was waiting to be sentenced.

Luckily, she had a great therapist in Holloway who really helped her begin to rebuild her life and regain her confidence. Gurmit was enrolled on a few courses and she was starting to rebuild and recover, but at a great cost. Having a criminal conviction would make it very hard for her to work in finance or go back to the level she had worked so hard to achieve in her profession. She was recuperating and determined to get some of her life back. She had been born to a working class and poor family, but her parents worked hard to educate their children and each had done well. I heard that Gurmit was sentenced to two years, she had to serve only one and so she was moved to an open prison near to her parents in the north of England. On her release she stayed with her family and worked for her father. She sent me an invite to her wedding two years later. I was touched by this.

Chapter 10 – Gertrude

All the black women knew about Gertrude, her case and the story behind her charge. She had been in several of England's prisons and had been in and out of Holloway, a couple of the white prisoners had attacked her when she was first remanded in Holloway because they had been told she had hurt her own children. This was one crime no one tolerated and even hated in a women's prison. Gertrude was sent to another prison in the north of England, but this made it impossible for her to see her family and the solicitors who were representing her. Also, the court cases were in London. She was moved back to Holloway, attacked again by lifers or women with long sentences who didn't care if they were further punished, moved to different parts of the prison and finally she was now back in our section in Holloway. She would probably stay in this section until she would be released. Here she was better protected and the few white women around her were wise enough to ignore her as if they didn't, their sentence would be increased dramatically.

She was a bit of a celebrity amongst the black women as her story was one of horror and the worst injustice imaginable. Gertrude had seven children, and one of them, aged seven years had told a teacher at school that her parents beat her.

Gertrude admitted that she smacked her children as her parents had done to her when she was a naughty child, but there had been no beating. That night the six children who were aged under sixteen years were taken into foster care, her eldest daughter remained with them after she was interviewed and told the social workers her parents had done nothing wrong, but the six younger children were never returned to the parents. After three months, police came and arrested Gertrude for child abuse, sexual abuse of minors and on acts relating to witchcraft. She said that she did not even know what they meant, she had never heard the term "witchcraft" and was totally confused. They told her husband he was to stay in the area for now and he might also be charged and arrested. Gertrude was remanded in a near-by prison and social workers proceeded to have her children made wards of the court. Due to the seriousness of the charges, Gertrude and her husband were never allowed to see the children. Gertrude said she thought she was going mad when hearing what she was being accused of, what was being said about her and her family. The media just loved the case and reported utter lies or exaggerated or sensationalised the claims in her court case, about her family and her Nigerian community.

Gertrude had the worst legal aid solicitor, she was in her early twenties, newly qualified and Gertrude described her as being pretty useless. Nothing her solicitor said made any sense, and she never really asked Gertrude anything except telling her that she had to get her husband to sell the house as she did not qualify for legal aid and her fees would need paying. Gertrude refused to do this, prayed and thought, *This is all a mistake and the good Lord would resolve her hardships.* Gertrude did nothing, she was not going to lose the home she and her husband had worked so hard for.

The children's case, meanwhile, went rapidly through the family court, even though no criminal case had yet been undertaken and nothing was proved. She never went to these hearings as she was locked up for the criminal charges, but her husband and eldest child were there.

Gertrude's second oldest child was aged fourteen years and he ran away from every foster parent and home he was placed in. He returned home every time, until they warned him that if he continued to do this his father would be in even more trouble, so he ran away and slept on the streets. He then got into trouble with the police, and her son who had been top of his class has never completed school, spent a few months in a young offenders' institute and eventually returned to his father and older sister when he turned sixteen years. Similarly, her eldest daughter spent all her energy trying to help her parents understand what was happening even though she had little comprehension of what was actually happening. She tried to register herself as the carer for her siblings in order to get them back by acting as their foster carer, but the social workers labelled her an angry teenager and said she was not suitable to have them back. Very soon, the court gave the social workers permission to have the youngest of the children adopted. This was done covertly as the social workers did not want the older children to try to make any contact with their five brothers and sisters. The parents and two oldest children never saw the younger children again.

Gertrude was in her forties, but looked and behaved like an 80-year-old or older. She was now disabled and could hardly walk, she had ulcers, lost weight and had muscle wastage so used a wheelchair and crutches. They had tried to implicate her husband, he had managed to leave England and was now in Nigeria, the British police were trying to get him extradited back to England. All this had delayed and delayed Gertrude's case. Her two eldest children visited regularly. They were lovely children, broken, but managing to stay sane and the son was no longer getting into trouble, but working in a local supermarket. Her daughter worked in McDonalds. Gertrude had had so much hope for her children, and now she felt she had lost almost everything.

She still prayed, the other black women would come, clean her room, help her bathe and we all heard them praying and wailing together. It was a sorry sight and the noise was so sad and distressing. It took another two more years before Gertrude was released. Her husband never returned to the UK, Gertrude and the children visit him when they manage to save enough money. Her one great hope was that as her children reached eighteen years, they would come and look for her and so she will not go to live in Nigeria with her husband as he wishes all his family to do.

Chapter 11 – Nima

Nima was an elderly Burmese woman and she couldn't exactly remember her age, she looked to be in her sixties, but I guessed in reality she was in her forties. She had been hired in Burma, now called Myanmar, by an American ambassador about twenty years ago. Her English had been minimal, but she knew enough to get by and he had been impressed by this. She had been pretty, tiny, but determined and hard-working. The money had already helped her family move out of the abject poverty they were managing to keep their heads above due to her wage. She had found them a home and paid a year's rent with the American dollars she received.

A few months after being hired they moved to their next post in South Africa and he took Nima with the family, promising Nima a salary, benefits and fair treatment. He soon became a nasty bully in a country that Nima did not know and he kept her imprisoned in the kitchen at night. He had got her papers for travel which he kept and said that he was placing her salary in a bank account as she would need nothing when she worked for him, actually she never needed money as he never let her out of the home. During the day, Nima told us about her sixteen-hour shifts, she looked after the two children from the time they were babies until they left home to attend university, she cleaned the huge house and cooked. When the children were six or seven and at school most of the day, her workload lessened a little. They then begged for a dog and two puppies appeared. Nima was expected to clear up after the puppies and her small sleeping space now had to be shared with these two unruly animals that pissed and pooped all over her bedding and meagre possessions. There was a gardener and a maid who helped her, but she was not allowed to talk to them, though she did talk a tiny bit with them when they were alone. Nima's English was limited and the abuses she had received throughout her life were clear. She would jump at the slightest sound and would quiver at any television program that had violence of gunfire. I communicated with her in broken Hindi and bits of English.

Nima had travelled a lot, after leaving Burma, the family moved from South Africa, to Belize, El Salvador and finally back to the USA. Nima never thought to run away, she had no real experience of life, she was perpetually scared, fearful and powerless. She thought about her options, but had only been subservient and her psychic was reflected by years of torturous abuse. Then the ambassador with his family was seconded to the UK and after one year this was the time when the children went back to the US to attend university. The ambassador and his wife found some fault over a late supper she had cooked and he roughly pulled Nima into a car, she was taken to another large house and left to work at a friend of the couple in a house in Chelsea, London. Her belongings were not returned and she learned quickly that any questions would result in punishments from her new employer, even when she asked about her possessions and salary. Nima had no idea what was happening, and she didn't know where she was. She would spend four years imprisoned in this house. The family were not as cruel as the ambassador, they never beat her, but even the children called her stupid and said they hated the spicy food she cooked, even though she made such food rarely. Nima told me she was a great cook and had learned to make any cuisine from any country! She said she learned by watching chefs who came into the embassy to cook for the big parties hosted there. She continued to work all day and was never allowed to go out. She remembers a few weekends when they went away, but did not take her with them. They locked the house so she could not leave, but she loved this time alone and there was no mess to clear up. She could watch Indian movies and she just ate snacks; she gorged her tiny body on biscuits, toast and fruit so she did no cooking and the house hardly needed any work as nothing got dirty during those lovely and peaceful times.

One day Nima was woken up in the middle of the night. A man she did not recognise pulled her from her bed, pushed her and placed her roughly in the back of a car. They drove and drove and the car stopped and she was pushed out. It was freezing, she was left on a main road in her cotton night dress, and the man drove away. She was absolutely petrified, ashamed to be in her nightwear and unable to control the fierce shaking of her body. A few cars went by and eventually a police car came and she was taken to a police station. They were not kind, they pulled her and she started to lash out because she believed they were going to do something terrible to her. She was arrested and later detained in Holloway, she did not know why and she did not have the knowledge to understand and therefore explain to me what was happening.

Zoya and I tried to find out why Nima was in prison, but the officers were frustratingly unhelpful.

Nima told me that she had a daughter in Burma and she hoped she could return to her country. I tried to tell her that her country's name was now changed, she would probably find it very different if she returned, but Nima did not care. She just wanted to go home. Her abuse had made her hard, she got easily angry, could not communicate and I do not believe she ever had an interpreter called in to explain to her what was happening. I tried to help, but she got frustrated and angry even at me. She was a pitiful sight, she did not like the prison allocated clothes, she had worn cotton dresses and sarees all her life and she said she hated to be made to look like a man! Instead, she walked in her joggers with a towel wrapped around her midriff to make it look more like the clothes she was used to. She occasionally smiled and laughed when I made an effort to talk to her, but otherwise she was alone, solemn and confused.

Zoya and I chatted to various people to see if we could help Nima. First, we asked the Hari Krishna and Hindu priests who came fortnightly. We asked if there were any charities that would provide suitable clothes for Nima, and sure enough they came with two cotton nighties and a few second-hand sarees. The Hindu priest also brought her some religious icons, sandalwood prayer beads, a few Burmese treats, a few more clothes and sweets.

Initially I never found out what happened to her. She was moved to another area of the prison, even though the officers knew I was the only one who could communicate with her. She was losing weight as she hated the prison food and I was always worried about her. Zoya tried to find out what was happening to her, but she was told there was little we could do. I did write a complaint about her treatment after I was released, you never complained in prison as you found the officers turned against you and things became very difficult very quickly. I never received a reply to my complaint.

Zoya and I refused to give up. We decided our only option was to contact the Myanmar Embassy and if they refused, then we would contact a journalist in a newspaper like the Guardian. We went to the prison guards office and asked if they could use google and search for the telephone number for the Myanmar embassy. They told us they were busy and if they had time, they would do that for us. When we had walked into their room, three guards were watching something on the computer screen and laughing, probably at some silly meme or YouTube video. They were a lazy bunch, whenever you asked for help, they complained how busy and under-staffed they were and then they promised to get back to you, but they rarely remembered or helped, unless of course you were their favourite. They were busy for a couple of hours each day when the women were out of their cells, but otherwise what did they do all day? Zoya said she would try again, but I was impatient with them, did not suck up to get any favours, in fact I had been worried at Nima's declining health and the lack of support offered to her. It annoyed me how unprofessional the staff behaved and so I avoided them as I knew my presence would probably annoy them and we would get zero help. Zoya tried to get them to just look up a number for the Burmese embassy for us a couple of times, but the amount of time they wasted in telling her how busy they were less than equal to how long it would have taken them to search for the number. We gave up, I said I would call directory enquiries, a costly venture, but Zoya told me to hang on, there were people at the prison who were always willing to help. We were impatient with wanting to help Nima, but we thought together and listed all the people who might help. The trick was always to ask a range of different people for various help.

We decided to ask the lovely education teaching staff in computing to find us a contact for the Myanmar Embassy as they had access to the internet that we did not have. He asked us why we needed that and when we told him about Nima and her plight, he also let us use the office telephone when we told him that we were trying to get her help. He gave us some useful advice and tips of what to say, one was to not say we were fellow prisoners. I contacted the embassy and spoke to different staff. As advised, I did not tell them I was a prisoner, but I implied that I had met Nima whilst visiting Holloway. They did not seem shocked, but also not that bothered so I said that I would write to the newspaper as I had several contacts and tell them about Nima and how the embassy refused her help. Very soon I was put through to the ambassador's deputy, who was a lovely woman and she listened to me intently. She was genuinely concerned and willing to help. She gave me her email, asked me to write, explain in detail and give me Nima's full name and contact details. She was not phased when I told her that Nima was imprisoned and in a bad way. Zoya and I wrote exactly what we wanted to say, asked our lovely and helpful educator to send an email on our behalf which he did immediately while we watched. He typed up the information and sent the email that very minute.

The deputy ambassador arrived with two of her staff three days later and visited Nima whose full details had been found, they said that they had tried to contact the American Embassy about the ambassador who had abused her, but gave up when they realised this would not help Nima at this time. Instead, they wanted to help Nima get out of prison and maybe get back to Myanmar. They came with new clothes, sarees with blouses and matching under-petticoats, some underwear, warm woollens, treats, new shoes, and listening-ears. They spoke to her gently and in her mother-tongue. I saw Nima from a distance in prison and she looked absolutely different, she was moved to a nicer part of the prison and the embassy sent food for her a couple of times a week. Within a month Nima was released as she had committed no crime, so the embassy had been helpful and kind as they promised. Nima was given accommodation whilst her papers were prepared. Luckily, I was due to be released and went to see her before she flew back home. I packed a small suitcase with some lovely clothes, chocolates, what I thought would make lovely presents for her family and an envelope with two hundred dollars. Two weeks later the embassy called me and told me that Nima was on a flight home to Burma, Myanmar. They had found and contacted her family, and arrangements had been made to support her when she arrived back home. I wondered if Zoya knew what had happened to Nima. I am sure she would know, at least, that Nima had been released into the care of the embassy. I, of course, would inform her later of all the details in one of the letters I sent her.

Chapter 12 – Kerry and Sara

These two women looked scary when I first met them in art class. They were inseparable, you rarely saw quiet and thin Sara without the loud and obese Kerry. She approached me and asked if I smoked and without waiting for me to answer, asked me for a cigarette. She, at first, did not believe me when I said I did not smoke, asked when I gave up and I told her I had never smoked in my life, that I didn't even know how to inhale! She looked at me, laughed and then started to chatter, whilst Sara looked on and nodded from time to time. She told me how she and Sara had spent their adult life in and out of Holloway. Both had been abused and abandoned by their families as children. Drugs were Kerry's reason, she told me she did not remember a time when her mum was not stoned, the house was often cold, filthy and food was scarce. She told me how her mum brought men and puppies home, she would get bored of them and out they went. The puppies made a mess and chewed on everything, so all the furniture, clothes and carpets looked scrappy. The smell in their house was so bad that even as a child she could not bear it. Kerry told me about being bitten by fleas that she did not know whether they came from her own head or from the puppies.

Sara was first raped when aged 8 years by her mother's boyfriend. This continued until her mother threw that man out. There was peace for Sara for about a year, but then she had a run of different men coming in and out of their home. Several turned to Sara when her mum was either drunk or high on what they had given her. When she could no longer bear the terrible things, these awful men were doing to her, she ran away at the age of 14 years old. She had told teachers and social workers, but her mother and the boyfriends convinced them that she was a liar, a thief and was looking for attention. Sara could no longer tell anyone what had happened to her, and she had been left traumatised. When she ran away, no one came looking for her. She saw her mother once in a supermarket when she was about sixteen years old, but her mother turned around without saying a word and walked away.

Kerry met Sara sleeping rough outside Kings Cross Railway Station in London, and knew that she would soon have a pimp exploiting her. Kerry was not much older than Sara, but she felt motherly towards her the minute they met. She told Sara she would look after her. They had the best year. Sara loved someone caring for her, she felt safe and liked, Kerry knew everything about surviving on the streets, where to get food, a bath, where she could sleep safely and avoid the abusers. On the whole they bragged how good they were at shoplifting for food, sanitary items and bits of clothes, and purposefully got caught when it started to get cold as Holloway was better than any hostel. I could see Kerry's potential straight away. I asked them why they didn't get a place to live together and do jobs so then they could have the life they wanted, together and safe. Sara actually spoke up, you could see her passion and wanting to be safe. She told me they had tried, had registered an address in a hostel to get government support, got on various lists such as for support from different charities, and spent days upon days meeting different professionals, but were never helped to find permanent accommodation. They never got help to find a job, had to sign on for benefits and show they were looking for work to qualify, but had never been taught to use a computer yet were expected to use one to look for jobs and accommodation. They stayed in different bed and breakfast accommodation, but often these were damp and noisy, and Kerry would get drunk, was abusive and they got thrown out of these inferior places. Kerry found that these landlords were paid thousands of pounds to accommodate them, whilst they lived in these small damp rooms with shared dirty bathrooms and little comfort. It made her blood boil, so she would drink, become abusive or shout truths at them, and they would get thrown out and lose the accommodation. They felt exploited and that no one really cared.

Kerry was smart, she told me about all these charities. She shared that they had got funding that mostly paid hefty salaries by using people like her to raise funds. She said again and again how she felt taken advantage of and that this was no different to what pimps did. She described how once she stood outside Oxfam when it was particularly cold outside and saw people partying with tables full of food and booze, yet she had spent lunchtime begging for some tea and a sandwich. She told me how nice it was to get drunk, because it made it easier to sleep outside or in a squat when it was so cold. No number of blankets on top of her sleeping bag would keep them warm, or stop the damp hurting their body and so they drank alcohol to forget the hardships.

Kerry and Sara, both told me about the people who looked down on them, others coming and chatting to them in order to make themselves feel good about the coins or the few pounds or food they gave them. All they had wanted was to be safe and learn things that would make them equal to females their age when they were fifteen and sixteen years old, but instead there were so many regulations, so much they had no understanding of and adults were always preaching at them and setting more rules. Sara said it was a different kind of abuse, people feeling sorry for her, yet having no sadness when they went back to the damp bed and breakfast or the squat or under the archway or travelling on the warm tube until they were thrown out or the police were called late at night. She told me about all the charity workers they had met and what they experienced, a few were nice, but most were just doing a job and were patronising, returning to their fancy homes having little compassion for the likes of them.

The prison officers were not allowed to let friends and lovers stay together in one cell, but Kerry and Sara behaved impeccably if allowed to be in the same room, so this is what happened, luckily, to them. They loved the classes, were actually quite talented and if they had found the right official professional to care for them like this on the outside, I am sure they would have managed outside of Holloway. They were now institutionalised and actually loved being in Holloway. I calculated the costs of this and it was ridiculous. Kerry also knew that this all cost a lot of money, but they never had similar opportunities on the outside and no help to manage to live with support that they had been denied all their young lives. Kerry told me that even in Holloway, when they were released, they were never really skilled to survive on the outside, all they were given was a hostel address and the money they saved in prison, usually ten to twenty pounds plus a tube ticket to the hostel. This got them nowhere.

One day Kerry had a fight with Lizzie when she gave her a small portion, normally Sara picked at her food and Kerry would finish both their meals, so it was always enough. Food was hugely important to Kerry. Lizzie did this just to wind Kerry up and it worked, Kerry threw the food at Lizzie when she would not give her a decent portion and Lizzie smirked, and we all saw this. Kerry fell into the trap. Kerry was restrained and taken into isolation, and from then on Sara refused to go outside, she refused to get up, leave her room, clean it, bathe or eat. The prison officers and the therapist had no effect, Sara ignored them. After two days Kerry was released just so she could support Sara. As soon as Kerry came down, she picked Sara up and placed her in a hot bath, stripped her clothes and put them into the laundry. Sara looked awful; I do not think she had even drank any water since Kerry was taken away. Kerry never allowed anyone into their room, but Tsitsi had entered and stripped the soiled bed, Kerry said nothing, took the bedding and placed it with Sara's clothes, and put the machine on the hottest wash. She left Sara to continue to soak, whilst she wiped the plastic mattress and mopped the floor after disinfecting the whole room. Tsitsi helped and then left to do her own work. Kerry collected Sara from the bathroom wrapped in towels, dressed her and laid her on the freshly made bed. One of the women from the kitchen brought them breakfast, hot milk and gave it to Kerry without a word. The prison officer looked in and saw Kerry cooing at Sara getting her to eat a little toast soaked in the hot milk.

Kerry and Sara were released within four months, but we all knew they would be back the next winter.

Chapter 13 – Verity Prienz

Verity was a celebrity the minute she walked into Holloway, both for the prisoners and the staff who worked in Holloway. There is a hierarchy of treatment, allowances, the rooms and area of the prison women are allocated to. Verity was taken to the best part of the prison, and then again moved to an even better place, in the unit where the mother and baby are, an area where you have access to a private garden, a kitchen with microwaves and other equipment. A place with much more freedom and privileges.

The case was widely discussed in the news and many different programmes on TV. The women vociferously and loudly shared their opinion on what she did, why she admitted the mistakes ten years later, who was to blame and most of the women sided with Verity. There is nothing like a woman scorned! All the women had an opinion on the new woman draping her arms around Verity's ex-husband, a famous Minister of the European Parliament, MEP, during the trial as this new woman looked not that different to Verity! We all expected a young, beautiful and glamorous woman because Verity appeared to be very intelligent, academic, but quite plain-looking to all of us. The new woman appeared no different to Verity in looks, manner and behaviour, we were dumbfounded! No wonder she was so angry. Verity was found to be guilty, we all knew she would be given a prison sentence and as we guessed she was sentenced to eight-months in March 2013 for perverting the course of justice. She had said that she had been driving the car when caught speeding and it had actually been her MEP husband in 2003. He already had nine points, so three more points would have meant that he would lose his driving licence and get banned from driving. In 2011 Verity found out that her husband had been having an affair, was going to leave her. Miraculously his crime with her true role in the matter came to light about the same time. She was interviewed and admitted the truth to the police, she was then charged and awaited a trial. Of course, she was not remanded in prison. I think her solicitors thought she would get away with what she had done by saying her husband coerced her to do it and we were all impressed by a woman actually willing to blame the man, but both she and her ex-husband were tried, and found guilty. All the women in Holloway agreed it was a farce. Normally such cases have community service or a fine allocated to the sentence, but the injustice system had been criticised for punishing only the lower classes unfairly, so examples were now being made of the middle-upper classes, the rich and for crimes that were mainly white-collar issues. The cost to the public purse from the taxes paid by the normal person was extraordinary, but such examples were now being made. It was all a sham.

Verity was kept away from most of the inmates, she was seen in the library and in other privileged areas, then we heard that she was moved to HM Prison East Sutton Park within days of her being in Holloway prison. This was a much better open prison, and most of the women on lesser charges had been on a waiting list to move there. There was so much anger about the unfairness of this, and how had she managed to jump the queue, well we all knew why. This open prison was considered an easy option, where women were allowed greater entitlements, could play games, access a beautiful garden, were allowed much more freedom and home visits if they behaved well. There were women like Zoya who had requested and requested to move there, but was told it was full. It was totally unfair. Verity lost all our sympathy.

Verity had five children and one of the TV programs told us how the children sided with their mum and refused to talk to or now see the father, he was also now in an open prison, but his children did not visit. Her family were looking after them and Verity got to see her children frequently. Again, this was rarely the case for most of the women in Holloway and the discrimination and the force of the unfairness was felt by each of us. Worse was seeing her talk about her "difficult and terrible" experience in prison after her release, she wrote articles about it and even got a book published. She had been treated well and better than any of us. Unless you were famous, a football player or a so-called famous celebrity who had committed crimes, then they had similar treatment to Verity. After hearing her talk for a short time in a television programme, there was shouting, jeering and booing. Communal TVs had to be turned off, otherwise there would have been an actual riot.

She served only two months in an institution few considered a punishment. There were discussions about people saying how the legal system was too lenient, sentences should be longer and conditions worse. People complained that there were gyms and television in prisons. The actual punishment was the long periods of being locked up, of not seeing daylight and living with unpredictable people. Of the pain of missing children or totally losing them. If only the truth was known. I think systems in Scandinavia work better and there is much to learn from them. They have institutions where there is proper rehabilitation, criminalised people doing jobs that give back to society and disturbed or people abused when young or born with a deficiency are helped to get better, to improve and learn to live in society. Wasting money simply to lock people away and for some rich person somewhere to make money out of these people is no answer. Terrible murders and crimes happen in very, very small numbers, the majority of prisoners need psychological help and support or forgiveness. Also, the law is flawed and biased. I remember that every person I met from the uninterested police officers to solicitors and judges earned a huge amount, often smelled of alcohol from the previous night and, yet, seemed unconcerned about getting justice and delivering their work professionally. It appeared to us that they were playing games, the people involved rarely mattered as long as they won over a technicality or simply failed to do their job like many of the legal aid solicitors from apathy and a lack of care. I do not have the answers about how the injustices can be prevented, the situation can be improved and crimes that punish people victimised by others identifies and punishes the criminal and abuser instead. Should we punish the prostitute or the man using their services?

Chapter 14 – Aisha

Aisha was Iranian and had an arranged marriage, as was sometimes done in Iran, to a handsome and well educated British Iranian man. Aisha had only travelled to near-by countries in the Middle East and was excited about going to live in a European country, her husband was liberal so she wouldn't have to cover her head and wear the required Islamic clothes her family preferred her to wear in Iran. She was a stunning woman, with large black eyes, silky long hair and her figure remained girl-like even though she had had a child. Her husband took her shopping and his family were always buying her lovely western clothes, shoes and bags, they had helped her to set up a beautiful home, were always sending them home-cooked food and Aisha told me her life could not get any better. She told me that they had a wonderful life travelling, they lived in Kensington, and had lots of his family and friends living close-by. She knew she was the luckiest of women.

Three years after marriage, Aisha got pregnant and they had a daughter. Everything was and continued to stay wonderful. When Aisha's daughter was about three years old, she kept scratching her private parts, even her teacher had noticed this and called Aisha into the school to discuss what could be causing this. So, she took her daughter to be seen by her doctor and got her checked out. The GP thought she had an infection and treated her with antibiotics. A few days after, they had a dinner party which was quite usual. Aisha's husband was putting their daughter to bed, which he often did as Aisha was working in the kitchen. Her sisters-in-law were helping so Aisha decided to come to say goodnight to her daughter. When she entered the room, her husband jumped up. His trouser seemed to be undone and his shirt was out. She wondered, but did not say anything. The next morning her daughter complained about a pain 'down there' and Aisha decided to take her daughter back to the doctor and share her concerns, but did not say who she suspected. The doctor had to call social services and they came to see Aisha and her husband a few days later. Her husband was furious at Aishah for taking her daughter to the doctor with such wild allegations, and told her that the British social workers could take their daughter away from them forever. One of Aisha's sisters-in-law is a solicitor. He called her straight away, told her what had happened and she got involved.

Aisha did not know what to do, her husband's family were really angry with her, called her names and told her how stupid she had been to have such evil thoughts in her head. She wanted to call her family, but she was feeling ashamed and didn't know how she could have explained her worrying suspicions to them. She was even concerned that they might side with her husband as her father was very conservative. She felt sad, depressed and did not know what to do. She slept with her daughter when her husband had moved to the spare room the next night.

A week later, one of Aisha's husband's relatives came to visit and said, 'Let's go shopping and have some lunch.'

They often did this before so Aisha felt relieved and thought maybe things might get better with talk and support. They went along together. She dropped Aisha at the entrance of the shopping mall, said she would park the car and meet her in Starbucks. Aisha waited and waited, but her husband's relative did not come. She called her, but she did not pick up.

After another hour of walking around looking for her relative, and asking if there was another Starbucks. Exhausted, Aisha took a taxi home. On arrival, she went to pay the driver and her bank card did not work, she looked for money and had only coins. She gave the coins to the driver and told the driver to wait whilst she would get more money from the house. When Aisha tried to get into the house, her keys did not work, she pressed the bell, but no one answered. What on earth was happening? The taxi driver drove away swearing at her. She sat outside her own home and at 3.30 p.m. she went to collect her daughter from the nursery, but she was not there. The teacher told her to wait until all the children had left. She invited Aisha into her classroom and said that her husband had come with a court order and she was now no longer allowed to come near her daughter's school. Aisha asked why and the teacher looked coy, but told her to speak to him as she could not get involved. She left the school and called her husband, but the number did not seem to work, she went home, tried to get in again and sat outside. No one came. She tried to call all of his family and friends and found that her phone was now disconnected. She was really scared and panicked.

It was getting really cold, so Aisha walked to the homes of a few of the people she knew near-by, but none opened their doors. She walked to the high street. She saw the police station, went in and asked what she should do, and they called a refuge for her who got her a room that night. They were nice and helpful, the next day they got in touch with her husband at his work, he said he would come for Aisha, but instead he met a staff member outside as they could not give out their address and he gave them divorce and family court papers stating that he had filed for full custody for their daughter. He had accused Aisha of being mentally incompetent to look after their daughter, and accused her of having sexually abused their daughter.

On the first emergency court hearing held a week later, his barrister asked the judge to have her committed. Luckily the judge did not agree to this as Aisha had come without any legal representation, and he adjourned the hearing for two weeks to allow her to get a legal aid solicitor. Aisha had little understanding of what was happening, who to ask for help, where to go and what to do. Before she could do anything, she was arrested for child abuse and remanded in Holloway in case she ran back to Iran, even though her husband had her passport and she had no money. Her husband's solicitor, his sister, had made a serious complaint to the police of child abuse. Aisha did not attend any of the family court hearings as she was in Holloway all this time, unbeknown to her the case proceeded and the judge awarded full custody of their daughter to her husband.

I always assumed that refuges and women's aid would support women like Aisha, but no one really helped her. On her release without charge, it was again suggested that she had mental issues and should be committed. Luckily one of Aisha's uncles who lives in Germany had been told by someone in the community about what was happening to her. He came to Aisha's aid, got her passport and a few possessions from the husband, and took Aisha to Germany. He was so kind and told Aisha he did not believe a word of the lies they had told her community. The husband had refused to let him and Aisha see their daughter, saying that the child would cry and have a tantrum when he suggested it. Aisha never saw her daughter again. She and her uncle petitioned the court to allow even supervised contact, and they tried for 5 years, but during hearings in reports written by the court witnesses who had assessed her, the psychotherapist paid for by the husband, labelled her with words like, "she has a personality disorder", called her angry, said she was "self-centred, deceitful and dishonest", "narcissistic" and did not have the "best interest of the child" and all that the judge allowed was that Aisha could send her daughter a photograph and a card with a short letter four times a year until the child turned 18 years old. Aisha never saw or heard from her daughter again, she does not think that her ex-husband ever gave her the cards and photographs she sent for her daughter. She often waited outside the house when they were in London for court hearings and hoping to see her daughter, but the husband was living elsewhere and she never even saw her daughter from a distance. She begged the court to allow her to receive the same from her daughter, some photographs and letters when she could write properly and this was granted, but the husband never complied. When Aisha informed the court, they showed no concern and this changed nothing.

Aisha was heartbroken and knew that she would not be able to survive in London alone. She could not return home to Iran; her own parents were furious with the "mess" she had made of her life. She moved to Germany thanks to her uncle never judging her, she met a lovely man and married him. They now have another daughter and she is pregnant again. Aisha is one of the sweetest, gentle, kind and shy woman I have ever met. I can imagine her husband and his solicitor sister knowing all the tricks to destroy Aisha with their lies and unfounded accusations, and it worked in the courts. I always thought there were processes and procedures in place to protect women, gosh was I wrong. She sends me an email or two each year, but I never ask her much, especially about her past life and the never-ending court cases. We share titbits of news, she sends me photographs of her husband and children, and her art work, but otherwise I know little of her new life. I did search and read the court case when she was going through her terrible experience and the contents are shocking. The way Aisha is described by the judge is so flawed and untrue. Once or twice, early on she talked about the pain, a feeling close to bereavement for the child lost to her, she worried what her daughter was told, whether the abuse continued. She thought that she might be told that her mother had died because she and her daughter were close, and she cannot imagine how she coped without her. I wanted to tell her children are resilient, they do forget, but why hurt her unnecessarily? I kept my thoughts to myself.

Chapter 15 – Barbara

Barbara was a confused 82-year-old black African lady. She cried from the minute she arrived until they released her 2 weeks later. She had travelled home to Nigeria for six months, which she did every year when it started to get cold, and she was arrested at Heathrow airport when she returned back to London. She told us that a strange man had come to her house about two years ago and told her she would be in trouble because she did not have a TV licence. She said that she told him that she did not watch any British television. All she ever watched was an Evangelical preacher and Nigerian soaps. Her son had set it all for her and she said it kept her from getting lonely at night. The strange man who came to her home said he had an order to search her house, saw the television and he talked to her loudly. She didn't understand any of what he was telling her. She had bought her ticket to Nigeria as she did every year and when it neared winter, she returned home to avoid the cold weather. She spent the summers in London, helping look after her grandchildren so that her two children could carry on working over the long summer school holidays. Winters were always spent back home.

The enforcement officer had decided to press charges and a court date was sent to Barbara, but she had gone to Nigeria and did not attend the court hearing. She was found guilty in absentia, asked to pay a fine which she had not done and so was given a two-month sentence. A location order was served to find her, they found she had gone to Nigeria and all the airports were alerted that if she returned, she was to be arrested by the transport police and this is what happened. The cost of this would be several thousand pounds, as opposed to the licence which was in the order of £120 pounds. Barbara was actually entitled to a free television licence because of her age, but firstly she did not know about this. She did not even think that she needed a licence as she did not watch any BBC. Also, neither she nor her children thought to apply for a TV licence exemption since they covered all her costs as she helped with the grandchildren, and the mistake was actually the children's. What was done to Barbara was pointless and shameful.

The black women rallied around and looked after her the short time she was in Holloway. Every woman felt compassion and brought her treats to stop her crying and encouraged her to eat a little. Her room was cleaned by them when she was in a cell alone, and on day three she was placed in a ward where there were women of African heritage who cooed and talked to Barbara gently. She worried about what had happened to her suitcases and thought that they had been destroyed, but the other woman told her that they would probably be stored in the storerooms of Holloway. Barbara then worried and thought that they would take all the presents and food she had brought from home away and she was correct, they forced open her suitcases and all the food was disposed of, but her things were kept safe in the now damaged suitcases. Why had they not asked her for the keys to the locks? On the 10th day, an officer came and told Barbara that she was to be released two days later. She howled and cried. Her son had visited and sent solicitors, though Barbara understood nothing of what he said, he had spent several thousand pounds to get Barbara released, but at least she was to be freed into his care and live in his home from then on. Barbara cried even when she was on her way out. What a terrible experience for a lovely, old lady and who would wish this upon any of our mums?

Chapter 16 – Amy

Some women, actually most of the women stayed away from Amy as rumours stated that she was accused of killing her own baby. She had been in several different prisons over the last eight years, often getting beaten up, once to the point where she suffered brain damage and she was moved to Holloway, where she had a solitary cell that she rarely left except to go to work and, at times, when she needed something from the prison office.

I met her and we got talking in the library, where she worked as she loved books. She was shocked that I talked to her, usually only two other women ever associated with her. Even some of the prison officers kept their distance from her. She told me she had read and re-read every law book she could get hold of. She had an appeal pending as she told me that finally she had an expert in the USA saying that her baby might have died of the shaken-baby syndrome. I tried to judge no one in prison, except I never had much warmth for the women like Lizzie accused of pointless murder or the ones convicted of exploiting other women. There were two other women accused of murdering abusive men, and most of the women were less judgmental of them. I felt an immediate warmth towards Amy and I believed what she told me.

Amy was smart and she had worked all her life. She told me how desperate she had been to have a child. When her daughter died, both she and her husband had been asleep in bed. The baby usually woke between 6.30 to 7 a.m. and she clearly remembers being surprised to look at the clock and seeing it was after 8 a.m. She went to the cot and her baby looked strange. She went up to her, afraid to touch her and screamed to her husband to come quickly. She ran, got her phone and called for an ambulance. They thought that her baby had died from cot death, which was tragic in itself, but after her husband and Amy were interviewed separately then police came to visit them at the hospital whilst they were waiting to say goodbye to their beautiful little baby girl. They were both taken to the police station, they both started to panic and get scared. They didn't understand what was happening and neither took up the offer of a solicitor as they thought the sooner the questioning finished, the sooner they could go home and grieve together. Amy was charged with murder, arrested and remanded in prison at the police station and she never got to go home all these years.

Amy says she does not really remember much of what happened next, the never-ending questions, and the trial. She was not allowed to see her husband or any of her family as they were all interrogated and would be called as the prosecutor's witnesses. She saw her face in the newspapers and on the TV news, she learned that her home was sprayed with graffiti that called her a baby murderer, she told me that part of her died during this period. Her husband cried when questioned during the trial and share that Amy loved their baby and he had never seen her ever do anything wrong to the baby. The trial lasted 2 weeks and several experts talked about the baby's autopsy findings when Amy collapsed and fainted to have to hear the details being shared about how her daughter might have died. She is haunted to this day that they cut up her tiny baby's body and carried out all these tests on her. Amy told me that because of the appeal, waiting for results of similar cases in the USA, her daughter's body lay in a morgue these past ten years and could not be buried.

Amy was about 45 years old and knew that she would never get to be a mum ever again. She told me how she had known her husband since university. They married young and hoped she would get pregnant, they wanted a large family, and they tried and tried, but it never happened. She worked as a classroom assistant as she loved children and her husband was a painter and decorator. She told me how life was great, but she just could not get pregnant, but longed to be. They had almost given up, but the specialists had told them there was nothing wrong with either of them to stop them getting pregnant and so they kept hoping and trying. They had even been considering IVF. They started looking into becoming foster parents and had completed the initial training. Amy then found out she was pregnant. It was the happiest time of her life. She never felt sick, was joyous and well throughout. Her labour was hard, but she did not care, she just wanted a healthy baby and nothing could take away her immense joy. Their baby was born and the happiness continued, until that awful day seven months later when they found their baby girl dead in her cot.

All of Amy's food had to be prepared and brought in to her from outside as over the years she had found everything from excess salt, cleaning materials, hair, faeces, bleach and other disgusting things in her food. She was so skinny. She had a microwave and everything else she could possibly need in her room; her door was never left open and on the whole she would be escorted every time she left her cell. Initially a few women had tried to hurt her when she was in the library, but these women were banned from all classes, walks, treats and using the gym after being placed in solitary confinement, so such severe reprimand deterred Amy being hurt. However, the petty abuse, name-calling and threats she receives on a daily basis are hard to prevent.

Every few years when someone new came in and learned what she was accused of, they would find a way to hurt Amy. The prison officers had tried to stop Amy working, but this breached her human rights, and she was so polite and quiet, it was decided to better protect her, rather than punish her further. Amy occasionally allowed Zoya to visit, initially Zoya had worried and hadn't wanted to, but her heart is as large as mine. Zoya and I covertly chatted and passed treats to Amy whenever possible. It wouldn't have done us any good to be seen to be friendly to Amy. Amy knew and understood. She occasionally joined us in the Evangelical prayer meeting, Sally and Judith trusted us, so anyone we invited were okay with them. We chatted and had some snacks, we read and discussed poems or something we had seen on the television. I remembered the first meeting she came to and Amy was shy and refused our kindness, she wouldn't accept food and I told her she could trust us, no one had been "normal" or acted kindly to her in years. Amy said she had forgotten such civilness. Like Zoya, Amy did not reply to my letters, but got a Christmas card from her most years, but it did not gi me any information. I searched for her case and just ho that she was released and able to bury her daughter.

Chapter 17 – Fatema

She was a Somalian woman in Holloway charged with fraud. She was another beautifully dressed and intelligent woman. Fatema was tall, slim and elegant in her stature. She had studied in Yale, met her husband, a doctor, he was originally from Nigeria, but had studied and was now working in the USA. They came to England after they married as he got a better job. He was a charismatic, successful and handsome man, she thought herself lucky and wondered why he had never married and why she had been the lucky one he chose. he knew he liked intelligence and probably felt he married equal. They had a great life and both realised how nate they were, they travelled the world and ate at the staurants. They stayed in luxurious hotels, made friends rk colleagues and life was great. They had wished for

lives became complete when they had two sons. ed being a mum, they continued to have fun, nd holidayed with the children. When her eldest s old, the teacher called and asked Fatema to o his school. She had placed her sons in and they were doing well, behaved tema worried what could be wrong. She tried to call her husband, but got his answer machine. She rushed to the school. The teacher told her that her son had drawn a very detailed and explicit image of male anatomy. Fatema was as worried as the teacher who said she had to report it, but Fatema asked to let her talk to her son first. When Fatema questioned him, he said that it was Daddy's and Daddy had told him it was a secret that he mustn't tell anyone. She continued to gently talk to him and asked what he meant, that children did not have secrets from Mummy. He described things done to him and that he had been asked to do. Fatema realised what her son was telling her, that her husband had been abusing him, his description of what was done to him was very vivid and clear. There was no way he would know about the things he described being done to him. Her son told her that he drew it because he saw daddy touching his younger brother, who was three years old at the time, and he did not want daddy to hurt his brother like he did him.

Fatema was in deep shock, she packed a few bags and took the boys to a hotel. Fatema had no family, she had friends, but she was so horrified and ashamed by what her son told her, she needed time to think. Her husband called and called her, but she couldn't answer her phone, she needed time to think. The next day she dropped her sons at school. The teacher had asked her to inform her what she was going to do and the teacher agreed that she had to go to the police. She told the police what her son had said and showed them what he had drawn. Her husband was arrested and Fatema moved back home with her sons. She got the locks changed. He was released on bail, even though he had the means to flee the country, he tried to come home and found he could not enter the home. He came again and again, banging at the door and approaching their sons when they arrived or left the house. The police would not come to her help and she had to obtain a restraint order as he was scaring the children.

Before any progress was made by the police, her husband had filed for divorce and accused Fatema of being mad and took her to family court for sole custody of the boys. He had a lot of money, in fact he was the sole earner so he got the best solicitors and barristers, tried to have Fatema committed and the family court case proceeded quickly. Psychotherapists and social workers were assigned to the case. He kept describing Fatema as mad and mentally unstable. The judge hearing the case was called Justice Moses and Fatema told me how rude he had always been to her.

At the first hearing, when he heard the father was originally from Nigeria, he said, 'Oh I was born there when my father was working there in the tobacco industry.'

It was like he was speaking to a long-lost friend, they were very familiar, like buddies and friendly. Justice Moses was also in the newspaper during those days and Fatema wondered if this was prejudicial, how could a man undergoing a contentious divorce, fighting his own wife for property in a very public court case be impartial? He had been having an affair with a barrister, Fatema remembered how one of her lecturers had lost his job when he had slept with a student because of power imbalance. Should judges be kept away from the barrister who represented clients in courts, stopped from dating or having relationships and was this not an abuse of power? That barrister had been in a relationship and living with another barrister. When this man found out that his partner was having an affair with a well-known judge, he got into a confrontation with the police, held a gun from his window and was shot dead as a result.

It was all sordid and Fatema worried that this white judge was working, clearly struggled to hide his contempt of her and she found him to be very prejudiced and unfair. This judge had commented that women often accuse the father of abuse in such cases to get sole custody of the children, and so he ordered the father to have supervised contact. He said that as there was no proof of the abuse the mother accused the father, he would not prevent the father having contact. Criminal cases take years to be investigated and heard, family cases seem to run at a fast pace.

The father charmed the legal guardian who represented the children ordered by the court and she wrote favourable reports of the father for the case. Fatema started to become afraid, it was clear that the courts do not like bright, intelligent black women, but were favourable and charmed by rich men, whatever their colour. She had recently been told to read *Sons and Lovers* by D. H. Lawrence, here, the English courts always gave custody to the men in the past, often interred women in mental asylums if they resisted the man's abuse and to keep the mothers away from their children. Fatema felt little had changed in the judicial system in England, it was clearly biased towards men, and saw women as insane and needing psychiatric intervention if they challenged the man.

The system was antiquated and needed modernising, but the few women within it were more punitive than the men, they treated strong mothers worse than their male counterparts. Fatema knew that she was losing all her rights towards her sons. Until then Fatema had often got angry when she heard or read about cases where men were stopped from seeing their children. She remembered she had sympathised with movements such as "Fathers for Justice". Now she wondered, every time there is even a slight discrimination towards boys, young men and males, there is a huge sway in their favours, Fatema was surprised to learn how bad it was for women in England who needed help. She remembers the many lectures and talks she had been to that discussed the unfavourableness and discrimination of women in Somalia and other African countries and cultures, yet here in the UK the discrimination was as severe and bad towards girls, women and females.

Fatema and her sons were forced to be observed and see a court appointed psychotherapist who labelled her angry, inferred she might have coached the children to draw the images, and in fact most of the report was very negative about Fatema. The psychotherapist clearly did not like Fatema, he even said that she had tendencies of a personality disorder! After the second hearing the father was allowed unsupervised weekend contact with his sons. Fatema refused to allow this. Judges do not like women challenging their orders, he was harsh towards Fatema and actually shouted at her in court. He gave joint custody to the father; the boys were to spend one week with him and one week with the mother.

Fatema's husband refused to give her money, suddenly all the savings and money in the joint account in the bank disappeared, he said he used it to pay the solicitor costs, but Fatema knew that he had money hidden and property in the US and in Nigeria. She had trusted him to manage their finances, and with no access to his papers, she could not prove any of this. She assumed the courts did all this, that they investigated his assets, but no, she had to hire solicitors to query his accounts in a separate finance court hearing to do with how all the family assets were to be divided. She could not afford to do this and the courts did not help her. Her husband took a sabbatical, he said he wanted to spend time with his sons as she had denied him so much of the access the court had ordered, he said he was so stressed that he could not work so he had nothing to give Fatema, and she had to sign on to receive benefits.

She had to take her children out of the private schools as the father said he could no longer pay for this. Fatema thought she would really go mad like the courts had labelled her and she knew she had to take control of her life. Therefore, she started her own business, she realises she was angry and she was not good at hiding it. She didn't like the legal aid solicitor appointed to her for the custody hearing and she never saw the same one twice, so she felt her point of view or opinion was never heard by the judge. Not that he was prepared to hear anything she had to say, the psychotherapist had labelled her negatively and that was that.

When the boys were with her ex-husband, Fatema was visited by the police a few weeks later and accused of fraud, charged and remanded in prison. They told her a complaint had been made that she was claiming benefits whilst working, but she told them that she had informed the benefits office that she had started a business and had not yet started to make any profit. She had kept her Somalian passport as she had an indefinite leave to remain visa and status by marrying, but the police thought she could run away. She later learned that her husband had submitted a statement that said Fatema had been heard to say she was planning to run away to Somalia with her sons, so she was not given bail. The boys were sent to live

101

with her husband permanently in their house, whilst Fatema waited to hear about her fraud case on remand in Holloway. The man filed for an emergency hearing with Justice Moses. Her ex-husband was awarded full custody of her sons. Fatema also learned that her husband had bought the house only in his family's name and she had no right to the house as her sons now lived there full time. Fatema was angry at herself for being so trusting, absolutely stupid in the way she never checked their finances and had let her ex-husband take total control of her life and money.

Fatema had been in Holloway for over a year waiting for her fraud case to proceed, her ex-husband refused to bring her sons to visit her, saying that he felt this would be detrimental to their mental health and the court appointed guardian for the two boys agreed with the father. The older son was allowed to send a card to her once a month. He wrote how he missed her and wanted to see her. No one listened to his wishes. Fatema sent cards and wrote back to her sons, unsure if they would ever be given her letters.

I recently heard from Fatema, she had been released after her court trial where she was found guilty, been sentenced to 2 years, but she was released on time spent and good behaviour with an ankle tag. This meant she could go anywhere from 7 a.m. to 7 p.m., but after that she had to stay in her Housing Association flat. The tag was due to come off soon. She had managed to get her brother over from Canada where he worked, was married and had a family, an educated and wealthy man, who helped her with her family case and to get the flat. She had hated to ask for his help as she was proud and had always been independent, but now she was pleased she had asked and he had come to help. She was due to have contact with her sons in her flat. She was pleased that her case had been moved from Justice Moses to another judge, she had complained about him whilst in prison. Luckily the older son had never stopped asking to see her, which could not be ignored by the guardian representing his wishes, he was now almost eleven years old and articulate in wanting to see his mummy. He had asked to attend and speak in the court hearing about contact, and luckily this new judge listened to this eloquent and sensible little boy who kept saying he wanted his mummy. The younger son was also taken along to a contact centre for the first few months when she was allowed supervised contact with them. Her older son flung himself into her arms, the younger son was shy, but he watched and trusted his brother and soon went to join mother and brother with the games they were playing. He did not move when Fatema stroked his arm and hair, he looked up at her and gave her a shy smile. Fatema had six months of supervised contact every other week for two separate days and after her last court hearing, it was decided that the guardian would bring the boys to visit Fatema in her flat. This had gone well and she was hoping to see her sons for weekend visits.

Chapter 18 – Elena

Everyone called her Leeny, she did not talk to me, but Zoya told me her story when she was sent to isolation and a young black police officer was sacked at the same time that this happened. Rumours and gossip were of course rife during this time in the prison, women liked to talk and gossip. I listened, but made no comments. I knew nothing and I never joined in the tittle tattle, I preferred to talk one to one or to my small group of trusty friends in our covert meetings.

Leeny was always dirty, had to be told to clean her area of the room she shared with five other African and Caribbean women and to have a shower every day, although she always lied that she had had one and she rarely actually bothered to bathe. She was always getting into trouble, stealing anything she liked or food or treats such as the sweets and chocolates of other women, had a vile temper that matched her foul language skills. She had spent her life in and out of young offenders and then Hollway when she turned eighteen. She swore at judges, clawed and verbally abused the police, other prisoners and prison officers. She was always arguing and shouting at someone. Nobody wanted her in their room, she was moved around the prison, and when long term prisoners saw her, they growled and usually swore abuse back at her.

We had all noticed her flirting with a young black prison officer, he was lazy and did nothing, but hung around the pretty younger prisoners. Leeny was a giggly girl in front of him, she hitched down her sweatpants to show off grubby thongs and tucked or tied her tee-shirt under or near to her bra. I never understood why they had male officers in a women's prison, never mind young and inexperienced ones. I wondered if they struggled to recruit staff and so they took anyone? I saw Leeny playing pool instead of cleaning when I walked into the common room and this officer had his body draped around and over hers. I turned around and walked out again.

A week later we heard that they had been found having sex in one of the laundry rooms. He already had two warnings and Zoya and I could not believe that three warnings were needed to dismiss a prison officer. We also could not understand how a man could want such a dirty little thing. Once Leeny came into Zoya's room when I first used to visit. Leeny told us about how many men she had slept with. Her pimp found, supplied and charged men who thought she was a virgin large amounts of money to sleep with her. In her work Leeny was taught and encouraged to stay clean, dress well and flirt. Her pimp made her dress in children's clothes, pretty frocks, white ankle socks, school uniforms and sometimes she was even made to chew bubble-gum. She described the men who used her services and she thought they could have been as old as her grandad, men in suits, men in their dirty overalls and men from different countries and cultures. They paid a lot of money to sleep with a virgin, she pretended it hurt, she let them do what they liked and acted as if she knew nothing about sex and intercourse. Some of them really did hurt her, she struggled to breathe when they were on top of her fragile little body and, at times, she was passed from two to five men in one night. She described all the different sexual acts done to her, all the positions, they forced her mouth on them or on their private parts, some urinated on her and others wanted her to wee on them. She described how some wrapped cellophane around her head and she thought she was going to die. She was neither ashamed or cared, she knew her pimp was paid well, but she never had any money, instead he bought her clothes, sweets and occasionally took her to Southend as she loved the seaside. Zoya asked her why she did all this, and she said because her man loved her and he looked after her.

Zoya had asked that she get support to help her off drugs, get general therapy and classes to help educate her, but she was told Leeny was on a waiting list. I hadn't thought I needed a therapist, yet I had access to one as soon as I entered Holloway, yet Leeny was never really helped to rehabilitate. She was nearing forty, but looked and acted as if she was eighteen years old or younger. Leeny did not like the healthy food served to us, so she was happy to give away her food for sweets or methadone, but most women avoided her because she really did smell bad.

Zoya and I did try and cajole her to clean, bathe and eat. Actually, Tsitsi was amazing with her, she chatted to her and got her to work next to her, she taught her how to arrange her things, how to clean, always called Leeny to the shower room when she went, chatting to her whilst they were in adjacent cubicles to encourage her to clean herself and she brushed her hair. Whilst Tsitsi was there Leeny was clean, looked nice and healthy. Actually, this is also about the time she slept with the young prison officer, so this is why he did what he did, he abused a prisoner who was clean and looked normal. Leeny flirted and he fell for this sweet-looking, confusing woman. After Tsitsi left, Zoya and I did our best, but we were not as successful as Tsitsi and Leeny was back to being unbearable, vulgar, smelly, dirty and argumentative. She had a five-year sentence as she had breached bail and been found guilty so often, so it was going to be a difficult time. Zoya had heard rumours that she might be moved to a prison in the north of England to stop her pimp visiting her, infrequently, but whenever he came to see her, her behaviour worsened and she usually ended up in solitary isolation.

Chapter 19 – Krastina

Krastina told us about the journey she had made to come from Morocco. Her family were so poor, and she knew that as soon as he could, her father was planning to marry her off to one of his friends as he had been promised a dowry of five goats, bits of furniture and some money. She did not want to marry an old man; she had told her father this and he had slapped her hard. She was hoping to go to France before this happened as her French was better than her English, but she ended up on the wrong lorry and was instead left in Kent. She had applied for a visa to come into the country using legal means. She and her mum spent every penny they had managed to save on the cost of bureaucratic paperwork, processes, and on advice from a local solicitor. As they had little or no success, she sold a few bits of gold she possessed and paid men in her town to help her enter using illegal means.

In Morocco, she packed a tiny bag, hugged her mother and siblings goodbye and left whilst her father had gone out so he could not stop her. She started her journey to the port on a local coach. Once there, she went to the address given to her to meet the driver. She had already paid for the link. At about 2 a.m., she and four others, one child and three men, were placed in horizontal chambers that looked like draws at the base on the back of the truck. She said she imagined this was what it would be like to be in a coffin. She was asked for more payment before she was shut in and the journey began. There were some air holes through which occasional light streamed through, but mainly it was dark and suffocating. She was told that they would be released for a walk when on the ferry, but this did not happen. They were told to wear a type of adult nappy in case they needed the toilet, they had a small water bottle with a straw and she thought she heard the child whimpering periodically. She slept on and off, and lost track of time. When they entered Spain, the driver pulled off the main road, opened the draws and they were freed.

She wondered how she would travel through Spain, but then two cars pulled up shoved the men and boys in one car, and she was forced into the back of a small car with three men, two in the front and one sat next to her in the back. When she tried to speak and ask a question, the man punched her and she fainted. She was so hungry and dying to go to a toilet, she just could not go in the nappy. After several hours, they stopped, the car drove into a gated house and the car entered a garage. The men got out and pulled her out, she was pushed into the house and there were more men and a woman there. She was led into a room and asked to take her clothes off. She did not move and she was slapped hard. The woman took her into a toilet and told her to do as they asked or they would kill her. She watched Krastina go to the toilet and told her to take the nappy off. She told Krastina to wash herself, brush her hair and make herself presentable. They went back to the room with the men. Krastina was again asked to take off her clothes, but she stood still. She felt more slaps and punches. She woke up in another room on a bed covered in dirty sheets, she was partially dressed in her bra and a man was entering her sexually. There was so much pain in various parts of her body that at first, she did not feel the pain he was now inflicting on her. She fainted, came to, lost conscientiousness and regained to find a different man raping her. This time she found that she was totally naked and had bite marks on her body.

She woke to find the same woman who had taken her to the toilet was cleaning her wounds, she helped her up and placed her under a shower dripping warm water. Her body was black and blue. Krastina could not move, tears flowed and mixed with the shower water, but the woman looked on. When Krastina managed to get out of the shower, she could barely move and the woman helped to dry her and put her in an old bathrobe. She took her into a room with five other girls, her age or younger. The women helped Krastina drink a sweet, milky coffee and eat some biscuits. They gave her an old pair of leggings and a tee-shirt and put Krastina into a bed. She fell asleep. She heard the girls moving and saw it was dark outside. The girls were dressed in sexy clothes, high heels, had excessive make-up on and they left. Krastina continued to sleep over the next two days, getting up only to use the bathroom and eat what the girls gave her.

The man from the car came into her room and told her that she had to work for them to pay for all the costs she had incurred them. Krastina looked inside her bag and all her money and her mobile phone were gone, but her few bits of things like clothes and photographs from home were there. He gave her some more clothes and shoes, the likes of which she would never have worn. He said the girls would explain what her job was, basically she was to be a prostitute and these men were her pimps. The girls, there were about twelve of them squeezed into two bedrooms, would be taken to different parts of the city and left to work the whole night. Krastina was told to dress in the clothes given to her, her bruises were disguised using make-up and her face was plastered with make-up by the other girls. The woman she met was in charge and was some kind of spy for the pimps. She smoked incessantly, never actually worked as a prostitute, but she watched and kept a note of everything, how many men asked for them, she pushed the women into the cars and made sure she was given or collected the payment herself. Krastina had been a virgin and knew little of what was expected of her, the girls were not shy at explaining what needed to be done as they knew that failure would result in a beating. Krastina did not speak any Spanish, but she learned very quickly, she earned hundreds of pounds, but they paid her pittance. She asked one of the men who collected her for sex to help her, but he instead asked her to get out of the car and drove away. Krastina was scared and luckily found her way back. She knew that without help, she would be arrested and sent back to Morocco, she was too ashamed to go back home now.

It took her fourteen months of watching and planning her escape. She knew where her passport was stored, the Spanish police arrested them every two months or so, released them only when the pimps paid a bribe, but the police checked their passports and kept a note of who the girls were. Krastina watched where the passports were kept. She saw that whenever the men, the pimps had a good night of earnings, they celebrated with drugs, drink and having sex with the girls. Krastina rarely got asked as she did not flirt and get friendly with these men. After one such party, she snuck into

111

the room, grabbed her passport, she had always kept her rucksack ready with clothes, bits of food and a sock full of money. If the punters using her gave her a tip, she learned to hide it under her feet in her shoes and never gave it to her pimps.

She was terrified she would be found out, her money taken or caught once she escaped. She quietly left the house at 5 a.m. when it was still dark, jumped over a wall and started to run. She did not stay on any main road, but went into a residential area, saw people waiting for a bus and she joined their queue. She took a bus and stayed on it until it went to the other side of the city. She then started to hitch on the main road until she got a lift to another city. She could hardly breathe, expecting the pimps to find her any second.

Her fear was being robbed or being caught by another pimp. So, she did not sleep on the streets, but used her meagre savings to pay for cheap hostels. She cut her hair into a bob, changed her looks, managed to get a few jobs and kept travelling towards the French border. She worked as a waitress, picked vegetables on a farm and was a cleaner. She avoided large cities, if she saw prostitutes, she would move away and as her Spanish had improved so much, she could get away from saying she was from one of the islands near Spain. She never trusted a single person. Men flirted and asked her out, but she stayed focussed and tried to find trustworthy contacts to take her into France. She was told she needed two thousand Euros to pay to help her cross the border illegally and she had more than this saved up. She sent five hundred Euros to her mum, kept some for herself and bought her escape into France.

This time she was in a section of a huge lorry cordoned off near the front and surrounded by crates of goods. It was cold, but there was space for the eight of them, five adults and three children from all over the world. They took turns to sleep and sit or stand and this helped to keep them warm. She thought she would be there for a few hours, was nervous, but excited to start an honest life and send money to her family. She had managed to buy a phone, called them and managed to change the subject when asked what had happened to her over the many months when she had not been in touch. Luckily her father had mellowed when she started to send some money to them and he did not mention the marriage to his friend. Her mother and siblings were overjoyed every time she called and spoke to them. The men who she paid in Morocco had told her family that she had crossed Spain safely and was no doubt busy working in France. If they had found out the truth, it would have destroyed her parents and worried her siblings. Krastina had grown and matured into a smart, beautiful and intelligent woman.

Krastina wondered why they had not yet arrived in Paris; it was already dark and they had not taken too long at the border checks. The driver had managed to cross the border easily. She then found that they had not moved in a while, she started to worry that the driver had been caught, no one knew they were there and they would die in the back of a lorry. She eventually fell asleep. When she woke it was pitch black, but she felt that they were moving, though it felt slow. She dozed off and on again, one of the other ladies had her head on her shoulders and her child's head was in her lap. She sipped water as she did not want to need the toilet and ate some fruit, sharing it with the others in the truck. They all shared food and whispered brief, muted conversations, having been told to stay as quiet as possible. Each was excited to reach Paris and start a new life.

Krastina awoke again, saw light and was in a panic about why they had not yet reached Paris. The lorry suddenly stopped, they were told to get off quickly, as their eyes acclimatised, they stretched and saw it was starting to get dark again. They were all confused, and the driver drove off, leaving them in the middle of nowhere. Krastina nipped behind some trees and relieved herself, the children and adults did the same. One of the women had wet wipes so they all cleaned and made themselves a little more presentable.

They walked for miles along the road, two of the men had gotten frustrated at the pace and stormed off. A man and woman were left with their three children. They had travelled from Syria, Krastina decided to stay with them, but it was very slow. They realised by looking at the signs in English that they were in England not France. They were confused, there was no town or city and so they kept walking. Krastina tried to hitch a ride, but she knew this would never happen with her and the family, so she said goodbye and hurried ahead. She nervously held out her hand for a lift. A chatty, but kind man stopped to give her a lift. She knew enough English; she had met some young people on the farms in Spain who had taught her quite a lot. Krastina was always keen to learn. He assumed she had been working on the farms after he asked her if she had come from Dover, and she shook her head; no! He dropped her in the next town and pointed to the train station. She thanked him, he had been so nice and this surprised her. She hoped all English people would be like this.

She had no pounds, only Euros, so she waited until she found a bank to change some of her money into pounds. She had about a thousand Euros saved up and was hoping to send half of it home again, but she wanted to make sure she had enough money for now to get settled first and earn a salary so she could send regular amounts home and this would stop her family from worrying.

After her time in Spain, Krastina decided against going to London and instead decided to stay where she had been left. She found a cafe and ate a hearty breakfast. She then asked if they needed staff, the woman said "no," but she told her she had heard that one of the pubs near the factory needed staff and so Krastina went to have a look at the place the women pointed to. Her luck seemed to have turned, the landlord liked Krastina who was polite, pretty and when he asked her to stay, she did not complain when he asked her to clean the toilets, wipe the bar, wash the glasses, sweep and mop the floors and put the rubbish out. She said she had only worked in a cafe before, he asked her about references, but she said she had been a student and had done odd jobs so did not have references. As he was only paying eight pounds an hour, he was happy to employ this hardworking, young pretty girl and he said he would take her on as a six-week trial and see how she got on. After six weeks he never mentioned the trial and raised her salary to ten pounds an hour as Krastina never complained, no matter what work and shifts he asked her to do. He offered her a box room in the back of the pub and said he had his family so she would be safe in their home. She had started her job that evening and she never looked for another job. He was nice and his family were wonderful to her, she was polite, intelligent and popular with the customers.

Krastina loved her job, the landlord was kind and decent, she stayed and worked for him for over three years, he paid for her to attend classes on bookkeeping, she helped him with accounts, orders and he raised her salary regularly. He taught her to cook the basic food they offered in the pub and everyone got on. Krastina was hard-working so everyone liked her. She always smiled, but she did not mess around with the men and worked diligently. Her salary was now good and she sent about a thousand Euros to her parents every few months which had improved their lives such that her siblings had found good people their age to marry. Her English was almost perfect, she made a few friends and the landlord treated her as part of his family.

Krastina ended up in Holloway over a stupid mistake, one night in the pub these guys came and were being horrible, having drunk too much after their football team had lost that night. They flirted with Krastina and asked her to go back to their hotel, but she ignored them. At closing time, they would not leave, when the landlord tried to get them to leave, the men kicked off, one hit him. Krastina went to help him and she got punched and the police were called. One of the men blamed her, saying she was flirting and they didn't leave when asked as they were waiting for her to finish work and go with them. That her husband, the landlord got jealous and hit them. It was all lies, but the police questioned them, they heard Krastina's accent and asked to see her passport which did not have a valid visa. She was arrested, even after the landlord protested and she was detained in Holloway and threatened with deportation.

Krastina told me she thought she was the unluckiest woman alive, she had suffered, but found such a nice place, a great boss and here she was, she ended up in a notorious prison. Zoya and I really liked her, she attended all the classes, was in the gym, and shared all the treats she had with us. Her landlord continued to fight to get her out and helped her get an immigration solicitor to fight her case. He set up a collection jar in his pub, and people always put money into it as she was popular and everyone missed her. They were trying to get her released into his care, she was willing to wear a tag, she had a home for this to happen, the pub and as the police had held onto her passport so there was no way she could run off. The harm she suffered in Spain might have helped her case, but she definitely could not return to Morocco after what had happened there, but she had been illegal and was afraid to share her story. Her luck had turned, however, and she had many people including her local MP on her side. She had a chance at least. She was soon released into the care of the landlord, she was awaiting her hearing, and until then she had a home, was safe and could work.

Chapter 20 – Emily

Emily told me how she had lost her formative years as a young adult in a Spanish prison. She had grown up in a wonderful family full of love, went to a great school and loved life. She studied, had lots of friends and with her best friend Chess, Franchesca, they had both asked their parents for an interrail ticket which would allow them limitless travel in Europe for a month as presents if they did well in their final year at university. Both passed with flying colours and so got their wish of a European adventure. They had been saving like mad and could not wait to spend a month away in various European countries. They had a rough plan, but adapted this as they went along, so if they liked a place or something like a concert was happening, then they stayed longer in that destination or changed their course of travel if someone made a recommendation. They had a wonderful time, got on with each other, experienced and saw so many great things from the city sites, museums, galleries, beautiful beaches and rural walks. They met interesting people and had so much fun.

On their way home back to England, they planned to take trains from Spain to London via France, stay with Emily's friend in London and then go home. Chess already had a job lined up, but Emily couldn't decide to take up her provisional place to do a master's degree or find a job. She loved her parents, but three years of independence at university made her want more. In Spain they met a group of Italian boys, they had decided to splash out for a hotel instead of the hostels they had been using on their last night of the holiday. They were men, rather than boys, good looking, fun and they liked the two English chicas they met in the hotel pool. On their last night, the Italian men took them on a boat, they swam, had cocktails and by 2 a.m. Chess suggested they leave as they had to catch an early train. The men invited them to stay a few days more, Chess said no and explained their plans to the men, but Emily decided to stay, after all she had nothing to rush back to England. Chess was really annoyed, but she left hoping Emily would come to her senses and return to their stunning hotel.

She texted Emily and, in the morning, when Emily had still not come, she did not catch the early train as planned as she did not want to leave Emily with strangers without knowing she was alright. Emily came back at 11 a.m. to collect her things and still refused to leave with her best friend. Emily said she wanted to stay a week more. They had promised never to leave each other like this, but as they had almost come to the end of their vacation, Chess reluctantly left Emily who was now fast asleep. Chess finished her packing and went to catch the midday train.

Chess texted, she decided she did not want to stop alone in Paris, but took direct trains and reached home 24 hours later. Emily texted her back and also wrote texts to her parents telling everyone what her plans were and they were not to worry. That day Emily packed her things so she would not have to pay for another day in the expensive hotel and went to stay on the boat. The Italian men were exciting, adventurous, generous, they sailed, swam, partied and then they said they wanted to go to an island for a few days and asked did Emily want to come along? They said their boat was too small to sail across the open sea, so they were taking the ferry and were happy to pay for Emily. She was so flattered and she said yes, "Vamos, let's go!" She packed and off they went. After they boarded the ferry, the police came on board with dogs that checked them and the luggage for drugs. The dogs sniffed Emily's luggage and started to bark. Emily had never taken drugs so she did not mind the police asking to check her things. Very soon they dug out a huge plastic packet that was white in colour. Emily thought that drugs only looked like that in movies, but here they were in her luggage. She looked for her Italian friends and they were no longer there.

She was arrested and taken back to Spain. There were difficulties with language, she wasn't too sure what to say for the police interview and kept repeating that the drugs were not hers. They told her she did not qualify for legal aid, but allowed her to call her parents on her mobile phone whilst they listened. They could hardly believe what she was saying as she was crying so much, the police kept talking to her in Spanish and broken English to finish the call, but she needed her parent's advice. They said they would catch the earliest flight they could and would call the British Embassy in the meantime and be with her as soon as possible.

Drug possession and dealing in them are seen as a serious crime and carry a heavy sentence in Spain, and it did not matter if you were a foreigner. Emily was charged with possession to supply because the quantity was so large. She had her fingerprints and photograph taken, her jewellery, belt and shoe laces were removed and she was remanded in custody in the police station whilst she waited for an "abogado" or advocate or solicitor that her parents said they would hire. She hadn't eaten much that day, yet she felt like she was going to be sick. She knew straight away that it was the Italian men who had placed the drugs in her luggage, and she wondered how could she have been so stupid, naive and trusting.

Emily was remanded in prison in Barcelona whilst she awaited the trial, the solicitor was not hopeful, such crimes were becoming common and the judges were not at all lenient. Emily's parents went back and forth, trying to visit her for the allocated weekly visit that lasted an hour. Money was an issue with the cost of the solicitor fees, travel and hotel bills. They had already spent so much money so Emily said that it was alright if they came once every month or two. Emily was given a sentence of eight years. She thought they had been harsh with her, but she found that thirty percent of the prison population where foreign women on the same or similar charges, mules and female drug carriers were becoming commonplace. No one listened to Emily deny her charge. No one cared.

Emily told us how harsh Spanish prisons were, even though the Spanish women told her how much they had improved. There were two women per cell. There was a lot of hanging around and being locked up. If you did not make an effort to get on with the cellmate, it would become unbearable and she did her best. Emily had a few different women share her cell over the time, but was happiest when she got a lovely woman from the Dominican Republic called Carmela, who had been a mule and actually made to swallow about 100 small packets of drugs. She had done it twice before, but this time one burst and she nearly overdosed. She was poor, had a little boy and life was so hard back home, jobs were scarce and poorly paid, so her cousin recommended her becoming a mule. After a few trips Carmela was hoping to bring her son over to Spain and make a life for them here. Now she had been separated from her son for over a year and she was waiting to be sent back and complete her sentence back home. She was the main earner, she provided for her mother and grandma after her father died. Her cousin had found her a good legal aid lawyer, Carmela qualified as Spain had a relationship with the Dominican Republic.

Emily had to work like all prisoners have to in Spanish prisons, their doors opened at 7.45 a.m., they had to clean, shower and queue for the weak milky coffee and two slices of bread. If you had money on your card then there was a shop where you could buy better coffee and snacks. This was expensive though, but Emily treated herself two to three times a week, she missed her cups of tea and her mum's cooking. Lunch and dinner were always potatoes either in some murky-looking water gravy or in a watery tomato sauce. It was awful. They had one snack either an apple or banana, and you accepted what you were given even if the fruit was black or bruised. Emily thought Holloway was top class in comparison and the homeless women like Kerry and Sara agreed with her. Emily lost all her puppy fat and aged in the Spanish prison, she was in her mid to late twenties when she was finally allowed to come to London to finish serving her sentence, but she looked a decade older.

In Spain, her job was in a textile factory. They were led there, spent all day sitting at a sewing machine or at a cutting machine. At first, she had a back ache, but her body soon adapted. They had to ask to go to the loo and they had a maximum of three minutes to go and a minute each side to walk there and back, they noted how many times you went and this was limited. Conversation was in Spanish, there was disapproval if you spoke only English and this caused a loss of trust and arguments, as the women thought that the English speakers thought themselves to be superior. Emily learned Spanish very quickly, it was easiest when she had a Spanish speaking cellmate. Carmela was the most generous cellmate, her cousin came every week and brought her whatever the prison allowed and always gave her money to buy a few snacks, which were always shared.

Phone calls could only be made to registered and approved telephone numbers and if the person you were calling lived abroad, then the process took longer to check and activate. Emily could not talk to her family for the first three months, so she was grateful when they visited. The time, stress and cost were clearly visible on her parents' faces. Her father came once a year, but her mum and sister came a few times. Chess visited twice. Emily tried to be strong, but she cried and cried during the visits. She looked pale and unhealthy, by the time she finished work and managed to get outside, the sun was no way near the prison yard, so she hardly got any chance to absorb the tanning rays in the time she was imprisoned in Spain. Carmela was released and sent back home to serve her sentence, but she also lost her chance of ever returning to Spain.

Her parents hired an English solicitor who managed to get Emily moved to Holloway, her parents had to pay and cover all the costs for this, from the return fares and hotel of the two

Spanish police officers who accompanied her, she was cuffed to one of them and he delivered her to the transport police in Heathrow airport. Once in London, the prison service took over. Emily had to come in front of a harsh English judge who allowed flexibility in that after serving six years parole would be considered because Emily had a good report from the Spanish prison, she never got into any trouble and had worked throughout her time there.

Emily was a bit foolish in Holloway, she befriended Julia, Lisette and their posse. Emily shared a cell with one of Julia's friends. Zoya and I avoided her because as soon as she met us, she asked us questions and we heard her talking about us to Julia. We were not stupid and had told Emily nothing, we were polite, listened to her talk and apart from being polite told her very little, but Emily tried to befriend everyone. In Holloway you can be kind to everyone, but you had to be careful about the group you chose. It was hard to trust and if women found you gossiping or being in particular groups, they would avoid you. One night at about 11 p.m., the alarm went off. There were always dramas in Holloway, but this time we saw the police and an ambulance outside the walls. Zoya came to my window as when an alarm went off, even she had to return back to her cell and we would be led out into the yard. This time there was no fire alarm, a prison officer had set the alarm as he needed help. I asked her why she was late and she told me she had been helping one of the prison officers who let her print her coursework and send it to her university. Zoya told me why the police and ambulance had come, that Emily's cellmate had beaten her up really badly and they had found Emily unconscious and covered in blood. We did not see Emily for ten days; she was then returned to the prison hospital where she stayed for another week. She had a broken arm in a cast and a fracture in her pelvis so had to use crutches, she had been kicked and hit with a kettle until it broke. Her face was swollen and covered in gashes. She looked awful. Zoya and I visited her as the women she mainly socialised with were all banned from visiting her. Emily was awaiting a parole hearing, but Julia had asked her to smuggle, I assume drugs when her family visited as she was never searched. Emily refused, and thank goodness she had learned her lesson! So, Julia's friend punished Emily. Of course, Emily would not, could not tell the authorities, but we all knew and understood what had happened. Silly girl!

Emily was moved to our wing in a single cell. She now kept away from Julia's gang and did everything to prevent getting into any trouble else she would not get out on parole. Emily was released wearing a tag ankle bracelet six months later, she served only a year, in Spain they would have made her probably complete the whole sentence. She still lost a large chunk of her young life and would have a criminal record for many more years to come.

Chapter 21 – The End

Prison makes you ashamed, shameful and filled with shame.
I thought that we, the women who had grown so close would-
be friends for life. The truth is that we never ever met again.
There were no Facebook requests, texts or reunions. I had a
few emails for a few months and an occasional note or
Christmas card over the years. I saw one woman at the local
market, she recognised me, but didn't ask or say where from.
We both knew, she smiled, we exchanged greetings and went
our own way. I did let one woman stay for a few months in a
spare room. She begged and begged, said that they wouldn't
let her out unless she had an address to go to. I said no, and
no again and again. A probation officer came to see me and
asked if I would help. Finally, she turned up one day, and
begged to stay a day or two, promising to go to her parents in
Leeds after that. She stayed six months, she said she would
contribute to bills, she bought me some flowers the first week
even though I asked her not to waste the little money she had,
but she told me she had savings, then I noticed that she had
nothing much with her. I gave her some clothes and bought
her a few essentials and told her to help herself to the food in
the kitchen. She said her things were in storage and once she

collected them, she would repay me back everything. This never happened.

A few months later, a letter came for my husband, then a parcel in his name, but there was something wrong with them, the name was not quite spelt correctly. Luckily, I got them first, even though she had waited in for them, but as they were in his name, I had signed for them and she did not know. I telephoned him and he asked me to open both the letter and parcel as he couldn't think what they could be. The letter was a credit card in his name, but the name had an error, a middle initial that was not his. The parcel was a designer leather jacket with a bill of £1400 invoiced to the name on the credit card. Of course, he had not ordered a new credit card nor a woman's leather jacket. I didn't tell her that they had come, but she kept asking me if any parcels had come. Eventually, I showed her the credit card and pointed out the slight error and asked her about it. I could tell she was lying when she denied knowing anything about it. I had already returned the leather jacket and cancelled the credit card, having told the seller that it had been bought fraudulently and we had not ordered it. When I was cooking, I heard the door slam. She left and I never saw her again.

Some weeks later a letter came from the housing benefit office, she had claimed and been given money for rent, which of course she had kept. I did not mind, but I was worried I might be implicated so I telephoned them that she no longer lived at my address. She bought nothing, paid for nothing, ate my food and wore the clothes she was given. I think she actually made money during this time, but I still pitied her.

Most of the lifers have had documentaries made about them and over the next few years, I got to see the types of women we had been locked up with. About a quarter were some of the most notorious female criminals in Britain. Normally such programmes never interested me, but curiosity made me watch parts of a few of these programs. They looked ordinary, these women were the cleaners and cooks in Holloway, outside they had butchered, abused and even killed babies and children. There seems to be a thirst for people wanting to see such documentaries about some really horrible and cruel crime committed by people in our society, I couldn't bear it. I watched a few, but then struggled to sleep, often had nightmares and worried about people like Zoya having to be imprisoned with such evil. Instead, I wondered about the wonderful and kind women I had grown close to, socialised with and with whom there was mutual care in Holloway. None of them deserved to be in a closed category A prison, and especially those women on detention. These are the women I often wonder about, most of all Zoya. I continued to write to her, even though she did not reply to any of my letters. She had three more years to serve, and she is the one I wish I could see one more time, but she did not even accept my request for a visit and got the prison to return the money I sent for her. She had been eternally kind, and yet had expected nothing in return.

Holloway was closed down in 2016 when Sarah Reed died after committing suicide. An inquest found that she had paranoid schizophrenia and had been unfit to plead at trial. Like the women I had met, she should never have been detained in Holloway Prison.